"One of the Most Important Books of Our Generation"

"The Coming Revival could be one of the most important books of our generation. I pray that our Lord will use it powerfully to bring authentic revival to His Church and spiritual awakening to our nation."

Dr. Paul A. Cedar
President, Evangelical Free Church
of America

"Few books I've read in my lifetime hold more potential significance than Bill Bright's *The Coming Revival*. I believe Dr. Bright has truly heard from the Lord!"

Dr. Dick Eastman
President, Every Home for Christ

"This is one of the most open, honest, truly earnest books you will ever hold in your hands. There are no literary flourishes, no 'sell' techniques. Here is the actual experience of a godly leader who has discovered something of great value, something he invites you to share with him—*The Coming Revival.*"

Ralph D. Winter
U.S. Center for World Missions

"This monumental volume is long overdue. I felt my heart saying 'Hallelujah' as I read. For many, revival is a shopworn phrase; but Dr. Bright points out that by massive fasting, repentance, praying, and obedience it can be a vital reality. My prayer is that many will read this book and heed its teaching; and that glorious, spiritual awakening may come to our land. I commend it fully."

Dr. Adrian Rogers
Three-time President, Southern Baptist
Convention

"Dr. Bright clearly articulates the ingredients necessary for revival in America. The book challenges us to be a part of what God has in store for the believer in these last days."

Thomas E. Trask
General Superintendent, General Council
of the Assemblies of God

"God has put prayer and fasting in the heart of his servant, Bill Bright, and he has shared the call to revival in this remarkable book. I commend it for all who long to see our country turn back toward God."

The Rt. Rev. John W. Howe
Episcopal Bishop of Central Florida

"Bill Bright calls us to the biblically-honored discipline of fasting and prayer. If we respond to his call, then we will speak more effectively of our Christ to all who are looking for redemption and revival in America."

Dr. J. Howard Edington
Senior Pastor, First Presbyterian Church of Orlando

"As you read Dr. Bright's new book, you'll get new and useful ideas on entering into sacrificial prayer and fasting."

Dr. E. Brandt Gustavson
President, National Religious Broadcasters

"I believe prayer and fasting is the course God would have us take; nothing else can reverse the destructive path of our nation. Dr. Bright articulates this well in his book. I highly recommend it."

Kay Arthur
Executive Vice President, Precept Ministries

"Bill Bright has issued a clarion call for America's Christians to repent, fast, and pray for God to bring restoration to our land. Every Christian who cares about the future of our nation ought to read this book."

Peter Marshall
Peter Marshall Ministries

"In *The Coming Revival,* Bill Bright has sharpened our expectations, expanded our vision for God-given revival, and delivered straightforward, practical steps we all must take to be prepared. The thoughts are fresh. The challenge is compelling."

David Bryant
Founder and President, Concerts of Prayer International

THE
COMING
REVIVAL

America's Call to Fast, Pray, and "Seek God's Face"

Bill Bright

New*Life*
PUBLICATIONS
A MINISTRY OF CAMPUS CRUSADE FOR CHRIST

The Coming Revival

Published by
New*Life* Publications
A ministry of Campus Crusade for Christ
100 Sunport Lane
Orlando, FL 32809

Design and typesetting by Genesis Publications.

Printed in the United States of America.

Library of Congress Cataloging-in-Publication Data
Bright, Bill.
    The coming revival : America's call to fast, pray, and "seek God's face"
/ Bill Bright.
        p. cm.
    Includes bibliographical references.
    ISBN 1-56399-065-2 — ISBN 1-56399-064-4 (pbk.)
    1. Christianity—United States.   2. Church renewal.   3. United States—
Moral conditions.   4. Prayer—Christianity.   5. Fasting.   6. Revivals—
United States.
    I. Title.
    BR526.B75   1995
    269—dc20   94-46680
                                                             CIP

Unless otherwise indicated, Scripture quotations are from the *New International Version*, ©1973, 1978, 1984 by the International Bible Society. Published by Zondervan Bible Publishers, Grand Rapids, Michigan.

Scripture quotations designated TLB are from *The Living Bible*, ©1971 by Tyndale House Publishers, Wheaton, Illinois.

Scripture quotations designated NKJ are from the *New King James* version, ©1979, 1980, 1982 by Thomas Nelson Inc., Publishers, Nashville, Tennessee.

Scripture quotations designated NASB are from the *New American Standard Bible*, ©1960, 1962, 1963, 1968, 1971, 1972, 1975, 1977 by the Lockman Foundation, La Habra, California.

Scripture quotations designated Amplified are from *The Amplified New Testament*, ©1958, 1987 by the Lockman Foundation, La Habra, California.

Scripture quotations designated RSV are from *The Holy Bible: Revised Standard Version*, ©1952, 1971. Published by Thomas Nelson Inc., Publishers, Nashville, Tennessee.

Scripture quotations designated KJV are from the *Authorized King James Version*.

For more information, write:

L.I.F.E.—P. O. Box 40, Flemmington Markets, 2129, Australia

Campus Crusade for Christ of Canada—Box 300, Vancouver, B.C., V6C 2X3, Canada

Campus Crusade for Christ—Fairgate House, King's Road, Tyseley, Birmingham, B11 2AA, England

Lay Institute for Evangelism—P. O. Box 8786, Auckland 3, New Zealand

Campus Crusade for Christ—Alexandra, P. O. Box 0205, Singapore 9115, Singapore

Great Commission Movement of Nigeria—P. O. Box 500, Jos, Plateau State Nigeria, West Africa

Campus Crusade for Christ International—100 Sunport Lane, Orlando, FL 32809, USA

This is a book on the subject of fasting and prayer. Written from a spiritual perspective, the book is based in part upon the author's personal experiences.

The author is not a medical doctor, and it is not the purpose of this book to address in depth the physical or medical aspects of fasting.

The author recommends that anyone beginning a fast consult a physician before doing so. There are some people for whom a fast, because of medical conditions, would not be safe.

To all believers who will join with me in fasting and praying for revival in North America and the fulfillment of the Great Commission around the world—especially to the two million for whom God has impressed me to pray who will fast forty days.

Contents

Acknowledgments

Through the years I have written many books and hundreds of articles. In the beginning of my ministry, I personally researched, wrote, edited, and polished each book, manuscript, and article. Today, however, my responsibilities of leading a large worldwide movement and my appointments and travel schedule do not allow me such luxury.

This book has been a team effort. My special thanks to the NewLife Publications staff: Don Tanner, director of publishing; Tom Winfield, researcher/writer; Gayle Anne VanFulpen, Michelle Treiber, and Joette Whims; Judy Nelson, Worldwide Challenge; Mike Richardson, former newspaper editor; and Lynn Copeland, Genesis Publications, who spent many hours helping me prepare the manuscript. Special thanks also to my associates Sid Wright, chief of staff; Dr. Ben Jennings, international prayer coordinator; Jim Bramlett and William Nix, two of my assistants; Earl Pickard, director of Prayerworks; Pat Pearce, director of New Life Resources; Ney Bailey, International Ministries liaison; Dennis Kasper, general counsel; Steve Sellers, national director of the Campus Ministry; and internationally-known evangelist and authority on fasting, Dr. Julio Cesar Ruibal of the Julio Ruibal Foundation, for reading the manuscript and providing most helpful comments. Thanks also to those who took time from very busy schedules to read the manuscript and offer encouraging words of endorsement. Finally, I am grateful for my beloved wife, Vonette, who joined me for the last two weeks of my fast and encouraged me along the way.

Preface

I feel a deep sense of urgency to share in this book what God has placed on my heart about the coming revival. I wish to make earnest recommendations as to how we can prepare for revival personally, as a church, and as a nation.

Revival is a sovereign work of God—in answer to sincere, prevailing prayer—in which He:

- Grips His people with deep conviction, repentance, forgiveness, and deliverance from personal sins
- Fills His people with the Holy Spirit and manifests in them the fruit and graces of the Holy Spirit
- Fills the Church and community with His presence and power
- Causes non-Christians to earnestly seek Him
- Ignites in His people, young and old, a passion to bring the lost to Christ at home and around the world

Charles Finney, revered as the father of modern revival, called revival a "renewed conviction of sin and repentance, followed by an intense desire to live in obedience to God. It is giving up one's will to God in deep humility."[1]

Who is responsible for revival? God, or man? Do you work a revival up or do you pray a revival down? What are the conditions for revival? These are legitimate questions that Christian theologians and laymen frequently ask.

The great and holy, righteous, and loving Creator God is sovereign. He rules in the affairs of men and nations. Everything in creation is under His control. He has chosen, however, to give to His children the privilege of working together with Him to take the "Good News" of His love and forgiveness in Christ to the world. In like manner, He has entrusted to man a vitally important role in preparing the way for revival. Whatever God tells you to do, He will give you the power and ability to do. The apostle Paul said, "It is God who works in you to will and to act according to his good purpose" (Philippians 2:13). God has given to me and to multitudes of others a desire to fast and pray, and to work for a spiritual awakening for our country and for the fulfillment of the Great Commission throughout the world.

During World War II, we were fighting the Japanese man-to-man from island to island with great casualties. With a kamikaze spirit the enemy fought fiercely, willing to die for their emperor whom they believed to be god.

American forces knew that when they invaded Japan, millions of people would die, and the outcome of the war could still be in question. Suddenly, President Truman dropped the atomic bomb on Hiroshima and Nagasaki. The Japanese surrendered and the war ended immediately.

In the providence of God, I believe the power of fasting as it relates to prayer is the spiritual atomic bomb of our moment in history to bring down the strongholds of evil, bring a great revival and spiritual awakening to America, and accelerate the fulfillment of the Great Commission.

On the basis of His Holy Word and divine assurances He has placed in my heart, I am absolutely convinced that our Sovereign God is going to send a great revival to our nation and world so that the Great Commission will be fulfilled.

God's Word admonishes us to "seek first the kingdom of God and His righteousness" (Matthew 6:33, NKJ). Jesus said, "Whoever desires to come after Me, let him deny himself, and take up his cross, and follow Me" (Mark 8:34, NKJ). In Mark 10:29,30 He promises great rewards to everyone who forsakes all to follow, trust, and obey Him.

I urge you with every conviction within me—yes, with tears of compassion and commitment—to plan and prepare for revival. I trust that what is written in this book will be mightily used of God to help you in your preparation.

Fasting is the only discipline that meets all the conditions of 2 Chronicles 7:14. When one fasts, he humbles himself; he has more time to pray, more time to seek God's face, and certainly he would turn from all known sin.

One could read the Bible, pray, or witness for Christ without repenting of his sins. But one cannot enter into a genuine fast with a pure heart and pure motive and not meet the conditions of this passage.

Prologue

More than six hundred Christian leaders, representing more than a hundred denominations and religious organizations, gathered in Orlando, Florida, December 5–7, 1994, in response to a special call to fasting and prayer for America and the fulfillment of the Great Commission.

Never in the history of our great country have so many leaders from so many different churches and organizations of the Christian world come together to fast and pray, to cry out to God for a mighty awakening for our country, to beseech the Lord to visit us from heaven with miracle-working power so that we may once again be truly a "nation under God."

It all started on July 5th when God led me to begin a forty-day fast for a great spiritual awakening in America and for the fulfillment of the Great Commission throughout the world.

On my twenty-ninth day of fasting, I was reading in 2 Chronicles, chapters 20 through 30, when God's holy Word spoke to my heart in a most unusual way. As I will explain later in this book, I felt impressed by the Lord to invite several hundred of the most influential Christians in the country to gather in Orlando as guests of Campus Crusade for a time of fasting and prayer. This would be strictly a time for seeking God's direction on how we, His servants, can be channels of revival for our nation and the world.

I was hoping for at least a Gideon's three hundred to respond. Instead, more than six hundred came.

God met with us in a supernatural way. No move of God in the history of the Church can equal Pentecost. But, in light of what God did for me and all who attended, this was as close to that world-changing event as anything most of us have ever experienced.

Many remarked how they had never been a part of anything so spiritually powerful in their lives. I mention just a few comments:

> This is one of the most exciting days of my life. And I mean that, knowing that God is listening to what I say.
> **Dr. Adrian Rogers**
> Three-time President, Southern Baptist Convention

> When God laid it upon Dr. Bright's heart to call together this gathering for revival, that was born of the Spirit. God dropped it in his heart. Now we have responded in coming and through the process of intercession and prayer, there is enough power in this room to move the hand of God.
> **Thomas Trask**
> General Superintendent, General Council of the Assemblies of God

> The gathering of some six hundred leaders was one of the most meaningful experiences of my Christian ministry. I believe that this event has the potential of becoming truly historic. Only time will fully reveal the many contributions that this gathering will make in calling the Christians of North America to their knees in humility, prayer, and repentance for revival in the Church and spiritual awakening in our nation.
> **Dr. Paul A. Cedar**
> President, Evangelical Free Church of America

> The fasting and prayer gathering was an experience like none I had ever had before, and the richness of it in spiritual terms was almost overwhelming to me.
> **Dr. J. Howard Edington**
> Senior Pastor, First Presbyterian Church of Orlando

I truly experienced not only a cleansing of my body physically, but a cleansing of the spirit so that I could have one of the most significant encounters with Christ of my Christian life. I felt a sensitivity I have never felt before in sitting before the Lord and hearing the Lord speak to me. I felt a more intimate relationship with the Lord than I have ever encountered. Barbara and I are both planning to be part of the two million people that the Lord has laid on your heart to join in a forty-day fast.

Dal Shealy
President, Fellowship of Christian Athletes

This call to prayer and fasting for revival in America and for the fulfilling of the Great Commission by the year 2000 may be the beginning of our liberation.

The Rt. Rev. John W. Howe
Episcopal Bishop of Central Florida

When leaders dare to come together and admit their need for a great infilling of the power of the Holy Spirit, great things begin to happen.

Dr. Lloyd Ogilvie
Senior Pastor, First Presbyterian Church of Hollywood

Through the years, I have been around churches that have prayed and fasted. And I have seen God do some absolutely phenomenal things. I know that when we pray and fast, it gets the attention of heaven, and God moves in and with His people.

Dr. Jim Henry
President, Southern Baptist Convention

I have a renewed hope that the Body of Christ can come together. I don't see anyone trying to hide anything here. I really believe this is a legitimate group of people who are broken before God.

Dr. Neil Anderson
President, Freedom in Christ Ministries

This is the most significant event I've ever seen because of the nature of the leadership that is gathered here from all segments of the Body of Christ—not just to preach on prayer and fasting, or to hear about prayer and fasting or the importance of it—but to actually do it.

Dr. Dick Eastman
President, Every Home for Christ

This has been one of the most wonderful, incredible times of my life. God was here and I felt Him. I will be passing on many things that I've learned here to women around the world.

Evelyn Christenson
Evelyn Christenson Ministries

I have really sensed a real sincere commitment to seek not ourselves but to seek God. And when you get leaders together doing that, then there is hope for a change. This is the greatest experience of my life; I will never be the same.

Chuck Colson
Chairman, Prison Fellowship Ministries

I'm really encouraged that there is going to be a major move in the Body of Christ because the headship of the Church is getting the right focus. These are commanding leaders and figures here. I believe it's a real sign of hope for the future.

Carlton Pearson
Higher Dimensions Ministries

I am sure these comments echo the heart-felt responses of all who attended the fasting and prayer gathering.

When reading the many portions of Scripture, including the major and minor prophets, we are reminded again and again that if we—as a nation and as individuals—obey God, He will bless us. But when we disobey Him, He disciplines us. Tragically, we as a nation have disobeyed and grieved God. I think primarily of the colossal insult to our God and heavenly Father when we betrayed Him and the trust of our Founding Fathers by removing prayer and Bibles from our schools. As a result, an avalanche of evil, crime, immorality, abortion, alcohol, and drug addiction has devastated our country and broken the heart of our Lord. This disintegration of America is not news to you because, like ancient Israel, our nation has for the most part forgotten God and failed to obey His commands (Deuteronomy chapters 8 and 28).

Our nation has become like Sodom and Gomorrah, only worse because we, as the most powerful nation on earth, export our pornographic filth and corruption to the rest of the world. We are not only destroying ourselves but are playing a major role in helping to destroy the moral and spiritual values of the rest of the world as well.

Adrian Rogers, in the opening address to the gathering, pointed out America's undeniably effectual role in influencing the world:

> I believe as the West goes, so goes the world. And as America goes, so goes the West. And as the Church goes, so goes America. And as believers fast and pray, so goes the Church.

Because of the moral and spiritual disintegration of our country and out of a deep burden of our hearts for America, we came together believing that the only answer was fasting and prayer. Although I was pleased to host the three-day gathering, the Lord had impressed upon me that this was not to be a Campus Crusade for Christ event. We were not there because Bill Bright called a meeting, but because God had called the meeting. We had gathered from all over America and several other countries because we desperately wanted and needed to meet with God.

"It is time to stop criticizing America and our leaders," Dr. Paul Cedar, president of the Evangelical Free Church of America, told us. "It's time to sit down in the presence of God and each other, to repent and weep over our sins."

On the first evening following a time of singing, prayer, and a moving message by Adrian Rogers, I lead the gathering in a private time of confession and repentance. We asked the Holy Spirit to shine His penetrating light into our hearts and minds, revealing our transgressions against Him and one another. We personally listed on paper our sins and then claimed God's promise of forgiveness recorded in 1 John 1:9. Our desire was to be clean vessels so we could pray more effectively on behalf of each other and our country. We knew that sin in any of our lives would hinder God in answering our prayers.

America is the greatest resource for providing more money, technology, and manpower to help fulfill the Great Commission than all other countries combined. So we know we are praying in God's will when we fast and pray for revival in America.

And fast and pray we did. We pleaded for personal holiness, mindful of God's Word, "If I had cherished sin in my heart, the Lord would not have listened" (Psalm 66:18). We prayed for one another, that God would protect us from evil and that we would humble ourselves and walk uprightly before Him.

Many participants also attested to the timeliness of this event in their own lives and ministries. Like Dr. Mark Rutland, senior pastor of Calvary Assembly of God in Winter Park, Florida, many wanted "to hear from God regarding issues in their own lives and about their future, call, and destiny."

We joined hands and confessed a lack of love in our congregations, our denominations, and organizations. Again and again, we found ourselves in tears as the Holy Spirit quietly moved in our hearts. While there was no dramatic, external experience as at Pentecost, God met with us in supernatural, life-changing ways. We did not know what to expect; we were simply there waiting upon the Lord, asking Him to do what He wanted to do.

As a result, we experienced praise, worship, repentance, unity, reconciliation, and intercession. We spent time singing, reading Scripture, praying, and listening to brief messages on some facet of revival and the Great Commission from thirty speakers such as Adrian Rogers, Kay Arthur, Lloyd Ogilvie, Pat Robertson, Evelyn Christenson, David Bryant, Paul Cedar, Bill Gothard, Peter Marshall, Jim Henry, Charles Colson, Howard Edington, Nancy Leigh DeMoss, Bishop John Howe, Ney Bailey, Shirley Dobson, Vonette, and others. After these godly leaders spoke, we prayed for fifteen to twenty minutes in response to their messages—all of which were related to calling upon God for awakening in America and for the fulfillment of the Great Commission.

Participants signed the following petition to the top officials of our government in Washington, D.C., affirming our commitment to pray for those in authority over us:

Declaration of Commitment

To:

The Honorable William J. Clinton, President of the United States of America

The Honorable Albert Gore, Jr., Vice President of the United States of America

The Honorable Newt Gingrich, Speaker of the United States House of Representatives

The Honorable William H. Rehnquist, Chief Justice of the Supreme Court

The Honorable Robert C. Dole, Majority Leader of the United States Senate

The Honorable Tom Daschle, Minority Leader of the United States Senate

The Honorable Richard K. Armey, Majority Leader of the United States House of Representatives

The Honorable Richard A. Gephardt, Minority Leader of the United States House of Representatives

General John M. Shalikashvili, Chairman, Joint Chiefs of Staff

And your associates, staff, and all who report to you
in your chain of responsibility and authority

We, the undersigned, as Christians having completed
three days of fasting and prayer for our nation (Orlando, Florida, December 5–7), do hereby acknowledge the vital position of authority and responsibility
that you hold in governing the United States of America and in positively influencing the world. Gathered
in the name of our Lord Jesus Christ, we have resolved to reaffirm our commitment to the admoni-
tion of Holy Scripture to "pray for those in authority"
(1 Timothy 2:1–4).

We wish to advise you personally of our firm commitment to:

1. Pray regularly for you and for those whom you
   lead and influence, as you perform your momen-
   tous service to America.

2. Pray that God will give you His wisdom as you
   make decision daily affecting the lives of millions
   of persons in the U.S. and around the world.

3. Pray regularly for your safety and well-being and
   that of each member of your family.

4. Respect and uphold the important office that you
   hold in the government of our nation.

5. Encourage others with whom we come in contact
   to also pray regularly for you and your family.

6. Pray for spiritual renewal and revival in the United
   States and throughout the world.

The theme of the fasting and prayer gathering was 2
Chronicles 7:14: "If my people, who are called by my name,
will humble themselves and pray and seek my face and turn
from their wicked ways, then will I hear from heaven and
will forgive their sin and will heal their land." As we fasted

and prayed from the evening of the fifth through the after-noon of the seventh, many participants said they were blessed physically as well as spiritually because of this experi-ence.

"I attribute any measure of success I have had in my years on this planet to fasting and prayer," said Carlton Pearson, pastor of Higher Dimensions Evangelistic Center in Tulsa, Oklahoma. "I don't think a church can exist in this satani-cally influenced society and remain alert and properly armed without it."

Kay Arthur of Precepts Ministries also emphasized the heart motive behind this discipline: "Fasting shows the seri-ousness of our commitment. When we step into fasting, we say, 'God, You've got to move. You've got to do it.'"

Yet, fasting is a new discovery for the average Christian. God impressed upon me clearly during my forty-day fast that He was going to send a great spiritual awakening to America, but He also impressed upon me that revival would be preceded by a time of spiritual preparation through repentance, with a special emphasis on fasting and prayer. I know of no better way to humble myself in repentance than by fasting.

God has led me to pray that at least two million North Americans will fast and pray for forty days for an awakening in America and the fulfillment of the Great Commission. I believe that as millions of Christians rediscover the power of fasting as it relates to the holy life, prayer, and witnessing, they will come alive. And out of this great move of the Spirit of God will come the revival for which we have all prayed so long, resulting in the fulfillment of the Great Commission.

I doubt that we will ever fully comprehend the magni-tude of what will result from the fasting and prayer gather-ing in Orlando. We do not know what God has in mind for His Church and for America. But we have every reason to believe that His plan includes a mighty revival from heaven. This was echoed by all present at the gathering. "America is stirring," summarized Chuck Colson, chairman of Prison Fellowship Ministries. "This is the moment for the Church."

As you read this book, I want to be very careful that I am not misunderstood. Fasting does not make one a member of the spiritually elite. One does not have to fast to be used of God. Everyone who joined us at the fasting and prayer gathering has had successful ministries. But there is no doubt in my mind—gained from Scripture, history, and experience—that those who fast with pure motives will be drawn closer to the great heart of God and experience a quality of life in the Spirit that is not possible apart from fasting. I want to be cautious that I do not sound like I am beating a *fasting* drum. I am committed to evangelism and discipleship. I am committed to the fulfillment of the Great Commission. But I am convinced that fasting and prayer by a large number of Christians will greatly facilitate and accelerate all three.

I try to evaluate everything I do every day in light of the Great Commission. Through the years, God has graciously enabled my associates and me to help train millions of Christians in discipleship and evangelism in most countries of the world. Together we have helped to present the gospel to more than 1.5 billion individuals and introduce tens of millions to Christ, for which we give God all the glory and praise. However, I sincerely believe that this greater emphasis on the discipline of fasting with prayer will enable us all to be much more fruitful for our Lord than we have ever been—and millions more people will come into His Kingdom and be drawn to serve Him than if we had never fasted.

I invite you to join me in praying that God will continue to use this fasting and prayer gathering as a spark to help set ablaze the Body of Christ in this most urgent and critical moment of history for our beloved nation and for the Church of our Lord Jesus Christ around the world.

A merica and much of the world will, before the end of the year 2000, experience a great spiritual awakening. This divine visit of the Holy Spirit from heaven will kindle the greatest spiritual harvest in the history of the Church. But before God comes in revival power, the Holy Spirit will call millions of God's people to repent, fast, and pray in the spirit of 2 Chronicles 7:14:

> If my people, who are called by my name, will humble themselves and pray and seek my face and turn from their wicked ways, then will I hear from heaven and will forgive their sin and will heal their land.

The scope of this revival depends on how believers in America and the rest of the world respond to this call.

The Holy Spirit gave me this assurance during a forty-day fast. I have spent fifty years studying God's Word and listening to His voice, and His message could not have been more clear.

CHAPTER 1

America
Under Siege

For several months I had experienced a growing awareness of the moral and spiritual decadence of our country. I felt deeply burdened over our nation's rapidly disintegrating values. And I was gripped with an increasing sense of urgency to call upon God to send revival to our beloved country.

I had a growing conviction that God wanted me to fast and pray for forty days for a revival in America and the fulfillment of the Great Commission in obedience to our Lord's command.

Since I became a Christian in 1944, I have fasted on numerous occasions. But I have never been led to even consider fasting *forty* days. That is usually regarded as the calling of Moses, Elijah, Jesus, and a handful of saints in the history of the Church. My own fasts have been for a day or a week at a time. Once I spent four weeks combining a weight-loss diet with spiritual fasting, but I had never approached anything that resembled a full-fledged fast for forty days.

At first I questioned God's call. For me, forty days was a long time to go without solid food. Furthermore, the idea did not suggest that it would be the most pleasant experience of my life. But with each passing day, His call grew stronger and more clear. Finally, I was convinced: I was to attempt to fast *forty* days. I was not sure I would be successful. This was a new venture to me.

I examined my calendar. Frankly, my schedule is such that it is not easy to find four, much less forty, uncommitted days anywhere. So I canceled several engagements and cut back on other activities wherever possible. I knew God was calling me to do this, and He would not make such a call without purpose. Because of this, I entered my fast with excitement and expectancy mounting in my heart.

Why such a long fast? I believe it was a sovereign call of God because of the magnitude of America's sins and the sins of the Church. The Lord impressed that upon my heart, as well as the great need to help accelerate the fulfillment of the Great Commission in this generation.

Decline Into Decadence

America is under siege. Tens of millions of Americans seem ensnared by an evil mindset. The evidence is everywhere we look.

Crime, abortion, divorce, violence, suicide, drug addiction, alcoholism, teen pregnancy, lust, pornography, fornication, adultery, and sodomy run rampant.

Airwaves carry sordid sex into the living room. Condoms are distributed to our children in the public schools. Militant homosexuals parade half-naked down the streets of our nation's capital demanding approval and special rights as a minority.

America is slaughtering tens of millions of its unborn babies in the womb and arresting those who try to peacefully stop the bloodshed.

Officials have fought vigorously to expel God from our schools. The Ten Commandments cannot even be placed on the walls of most classrooms.

Powerful forces within our country want to make it illegal to mention the name of Jesus, carry Bibles, display religious pictures, or wear Christian emblems in schools and in the workplace. They argue that to do so creates an "offensive environment of harassment."

As a nation, we have spent our way into a $3 trillion national debt. It is still climbing at an alarming rate, threatening to bankrupt our nation in the next few years.

In many instances, our state and local governments are accused of linking arms with organized crime by legalizing lotteries and gaming houses. They are joining the ranks of the largest gambling operators in the world.

Selfishness has become a hallmark of the people. Americans are growing more cynical and less compassionate. Their attitudes toward minorities, immigrants, and the poor have hardened.[1]

This sharp decline into decadence can be traced back to the day when secular humanism began to take control of our country. The level of America's sins would have astounded even ancient Rome whose own moral decay resulted in her self-destruction.

The Church is Asleep

And where is the Church? For the most part, it is asleep. Polluted with the desires and materialism of the world, she knows little about spiritual discipline and living the Spirit-filled life. She is complacent and at ease, thinking she has everything and is in need of nothing.

This picture is a mirror image of the churches at Ephesus and Laodicea portrayed in Revelation 2:1–7; 3:14–21, to whom the Lord spoke these sobering words:

> "You have forsaken your first love. Remember the height from which you have fallen! Repent and do the things you did at first. If you do not repent, I will come to you and remove your lampstand from its place" (Revelation 2:4,5).

> "I know your deeds, that you are neither cold nor hot. I wish you were either one or the other! So, because you are lukewarm—neither hot nor cold—I am about to spit you out of my mouth."

"You say, 'I am rich; I have acquired wealth and do not need a thing.' But you do not realize that you are wretched, pitiful, poor, blind and naked" (Revelation 3:15–17).

These pictures of America and the Church are but a few of the alarming snapshots of our nation. As I thumb through the pages of our national album, I cannot help but feel a sting of shame. Our great and God-blessed nation has forsaken its once-solid foundation of biblical principles. And much of the Church is spiritually impotent—void of a vital, personal, and intimate walk with God. Having fallen into the cult of the comfortable, the Church, for the most part, is no longer a power to be reckoned with. It has largely lost the respect of the masses; it is often the object of ridicule. Tragically, it has become the last place our nation would turn for help.

> *"It is time to stop criticizing America; it's time for us to sit down in the presence of God and each other and weep."*
>
> —Dr. Paul A. Cedar
> *President, Evangelical Free Church of America*

A Warning

Surely our nation needs a visit from our great God in heaven. We need another Pentecost! Many Christian leaders across the country are warning that unless America turns from her wicked ways, she will self-destruct. I believe America is under judgment. God's judgment is not coming, it is already here. That is why a tidal wave of evil courses freely across our land.

In Scripture, God warns that He will discipline His people and bring judgment for continued disobedience:

"If you forget about the Lord your God and...follow evil ways, you shall certainly perish, just as the Lord has

caused other nations in the past to perish" (Deuteronomy 8:19, TLB).

"Now I say that each believer should confess his sins
to God when he is aware of them, while there is time to
be forgiven. Judgment will not touch him if he does"
(Psalm 32:6, TLB).

A Sure Word

As I began my fast, I was still not sure I could last forty days.
But my confidence was in the Lord to help me. Each day His
presence encouraged me to continue. I earnestly humbled
myself and sought the Lord on behalf of America. The Holy
Spirit also impressed me to pray for major Campus Crusade
projects, including the furtherance of our *NewLife2000* goal
to help fulfill the Great Commission, to present the gospel
to every child and adult on earth, and to help introduce one
billion people to Christ by the end of the year 2000.

The longer I fasted, the more I sensed the presence of
the Lord. The Holy Spirit refreshed my soul and spirit as
never before. Biblical truths leaped at me from the pages of
God's Word. My faith soared as I cried out to God and
rejoiced in His presence.

Early one morning after three weeks of fasting, I received the assurance from God that He would visit America
in transforming, revival power. I found myself overcome
with tears of gratitude. There are those who say God does
not speak to you except from His written Word. Of course,
the Word is the primary means by which He speaks. But He
also talks to us by His Spirit within us (John 14:26; 16:13).
His divine impressions are always consistent with His holy,
inspired Word. God has never spoken to me audibly, and I
am not given to prophecy. But that morning His message to
me was unmistakably clear.

Anxious to share my excitement with my wife, Vonette, I
rose from my knees and stepped into our bedroom. I awak-

ened Vonette and shared with her what the Holy Spirit had been saying to my heart.

"America and much of the world will, before the end of the year 2000, experience a great spiritual awakening!" I exclaimed. "And this revival will spark the greatest spiritual harvest in the history of the Church."

Vonette was visibly moved. We fell to our knees, weeping for joy together in the presence of our great Creator God, our Lord and Savior Jesus Christ because we both knew that He had spoken. We were now sure that revival would come, and that our God had not yet turned away from America in His judgment against us because of our great individual and national sins.

> *"The longer I fasted, the more my faith soared and the more I sensed the presence of the Lord."*
>
> —*Bill Bright*

Obviously, multitudes of other concerned Christians are also praying for revival. It would be presumptuous, even arrogant, to conclude that God would send revival because of my prayers alone. My desire in this book is simply to share what God said to me.

Each day His assurances grew stronger, confirming the original impression that all the things I was praying for would be fulfilled. As I continued to wait upon God, I experienced the joy of the Lord as never before.

Shortly before I reached the fortieth day of my fast, the Holy Spirit spoke to me in another tone. It seemed that God was now saying that His promise of revival was conditional.

I have spent fifty years studying God's Word and listening to His voice, and His message that day could not have been more clear.

CHAPTER 2

God's Call to America

As I knelt before the Lord at my favorite chair in our living room, I was sobered by the conditions that the Holy Spirit had placed on His promise to send revival. These conditions seemed to match the spirit of 2 Chronicles 7:14:

> If my people, who are called by my name, will humble themselves and pray and seek my face and turn from their wicked ways, then will I hear from heaven and will forgive their sin and will heal their land.

With this Scripture strongly in my mind, I sensed the Holy Spirit was telling me that millions of believers must seek God with all of their hearts in fasting and prayer before He will intervene to save America. I was impressed by the Spirit to pray that two million believers will humble themselves by seeking God in forty-day fasts.

Again, I was duly impressed that God requires this great degree of seeking because of the desperate spiritual condition of our country.

But then I wondered: *How do you get millions of people to fast and pray? How do you persuade them to do this, perhaps just for a day or two, when the Church as a whole has lost the discipline of fasting?*

Searching for Guidance

For several weeks before I had begun my fast, I had sought information from medical doctors and Christian leaders to prepare myself. My search was fruitless. I found only two people who had fasted forty days—one in Korea, our national director and beloved friend, Dr. Joon Gon Kim; and Dr. Julio Cesar Ruibal in Colombia, an internationally-known evangelist with post-graduate studies in health.

When I couldn't find any material on how to conduct such an extended fast, I sought the Lord's wisdom because I didn't know what to do. I said, "Lord, I know You've called me to fast for forty days, but I can't find the help I need. I don't want to do anything foolish. I don't want to destroy my body. It is Your temple. Please help me!"

While I was seeking His guidance, something extraordinary happened. I distinctly sensed a sobbing in my spirit and, amazingly, I knew our Lord was weeping. I was startled at first. And although I did not know why He was weeping, I began to sob, too.

Then I sensed Him saying, "My people have forgotten one of the most important disciplines of the Christian life, the major key to revival." And I knew He meant fasting with prayer.

We can pray, witness, read the Word of God diligently, attend church, be active for Christ, and aggressively do things to honor the Lord—all of which are commendable. But the major key to meeting the conditions of 2 Chronicles 7:14, the Holy Spirit was saying, is fasting. Certainly, we cannot fast and pray for a prolonged period of time without humbling ourselves and turning from our wicked ways.

Now, in answer to my question about how to persuade millions to fast, I felt the Holy Spirit saying to me that this was *His* responsibility, not mine; that He will draw people to repent, fast, and pray. And something even more amazing: that He will lead the two million to fast forty days; that He will give them the desire and ability to do it. My responsibility was to love Him with all of my heart, soul, and mind; to pray; to share my own fasting experiences, trust His promises, and obey His commandments; and He would do the rest.

I had to wonder if I was hearing Him correctly. However, by this time I was nearing the end of my own forty-day fast, and I was now confident that if I could fast for forty days, anyone who hungers and thirsts after righteousness could successfully do so as well. I knew I was not advocating a new badge of spirituality, but a new burning of the Holy Spirit.

My mind was swirling with the realization that God Himself will move His people to fast. I began to see that this revival will actually be a sovereign move of God. That He is not through with America. That He still has plans for our beloved country. My heart nearly burst with thanksgiving and praise to the Lord. As my eyes filled with tears, I knew I had to do all that I could to relay this message to the Christian world.

Then the Lord showed me how to communicate this message.

Calling a Fast

On the twenty-ninth day of my fast, as I was reading 2 Chronicles 28 through 30, I was reminded of the spiritual decadence of Judah, resulting from the reign of the evil King Ahaz. As you remember, he nailed the door to the temple shut so that no one could worship there. He made altars to the heathen gods in every corner of Jerusalem and every city of Judah. It was a terrible time for Judah, from whence the Lion of that tribe, our Lord the promised Messiah, would eventually come.

Ahaz so offended the Lord that He "handed him over" to the king of Syria. The Syrian army defeated Ahaz, taking many of his people as prisoners back to Damascus (2 Chronicles 28:5,6). The king of Israel also attacked, killing more than 120,000 of Judah's soldiers, and carrying off 200,000 wives, sons, and daughters.

When Ahaz died, he was dishonored. He was buried in Jerusalem, but not in the tombs of the kings. His son, Hezekiah, having escaped his father's human sacrifices, came to the throne at the age of twenty.

In the first month of his reign, King Hezekiah reopened and cleansed the temple. Then he sent letters throughout Judah and Israel, calling all true worshipers of God to come to Jerusalem for the annual Passover celebration.

Hezekiah said this to the people:

> Our fathers were unfaithful; they did evil in the eyes of the Lord our God and forsook him...Therefore the anger of the Lord has fallen on Judah and Jerusalem; he has made them an object of dread and horror and scorn, as you can see with your own eyes. This is why our fathers have fallen by the sword and why our sons and daughters and our wives are in captivity. Now I intend to make a covenant with the Lord, the God of Israel, so that his fierce anger will turn away from us (2 Chronicles 29:6–10).

And he pleaded with them:

> People of Israel, return to the Lord, the God of Abraham, Isaac and Israel, that he may return to you who are left, who have escaped from the hand of the kings of Assyria. Do not be like your fathers and brothers, who were unfaithful to the Lord, the God of their fathers, so that he made them an object of horror, as you see. Do not be stiff-necked, as your fathers were; submit to the Lord. Come to the sanctuary, which he has consecrated forever. Serve the Lord your God, so that his fierce anger will turn away from you. If you return to the Lord, then your brothers and your children will be shown compassion by their captors and will come back to this land, for the Lord your God is gracious and compassionate. He will not turn his face from you if you return to him (2 Chronicles 30:6–9).

The wonderful results of their Passover celebration are also recorded:

> The entire assembly of Judah rejoiced, along with the priests and Levites and all who had assembled from Israel, including the aliens who had come from Israel and those who lived in Judah. There was great joy in Jerusalem, for since the days of Solomon son of David king of Israel there had been nothing like this in Jerusalem. The priests and the Levites stood to bless the people, and God heard them, for their prayer reached heaven, his holy dwelling place (2 Chronicles 30:25–27).

God's favor returned that day. He prospered the king and the people. But something special had caught my eye. Hezekiah *wrote letters* inviting the people to come to Jerusalem to celebrate the Passover.

In their book *Experiencing God*, Henry Blackaby and Claude King said, "When God gets ready to do something, He reveals to a person or His people what He is going to do...When God spoke, they knew it was God. They knew what God was saying. They knew what they were to do in response."[1] Reading about Hezekiah's letters, I knew just as surely what God wanted *me* to do.

I felt strongly impressed to write letters to several hundred of the most influential Christians in the country, inviting them to Orlando, Florida, as guests of Campus Crusade to fast and pray. It would be strictly a time for seeking God's direction on how we, His servants, can be channels of revival for our nation and for the world.

I am absolutely convinced that if believers truly love God, trust His promises, and obey His commands, He will fight our battles for us and once again we will be a nation under the rule of God.

When the Holy Spirit spoke to me about writing the letter, I was at home kneeling at my bedside. I called to Vonette. As she joined me, I read her the passage in 2

Chronicles 28 through 30 and told her what I believed God was urging me to do. We began to pray and weep because we both sensed that God had spoken to me again. I knew then what my first step would be: To help spread God's call to America to repent, fast, pray, and seek God's face, I must write letters to hundreds of influential Christian leaders.

Vonette and I had heard our beloved, long-time friend Dr. Adrian Rogers, pastor of Bellevue Baptist—a super-church in Memphis, Tennessee—deliver a moving, inspiring message of worldwide importance on television the previous Sunday afternoon. She suggested that I call him because Adrian would be discerning and his counsel would be helpful in how I was to proceed with my letter writing. I dialed his number and, after exchanging a few pleasantries, came to the point.

> *"When God gets ready to do something, He reveals to a person or His people what He is going to do."*
>
> —*Henry Blackaby*
> *in* Experiencing God

"Adrian, listen to what I believe God has said to me." As I related the events of the last hour and how I believed God was impressing me to write the letter, he grew excited and encouraged me to get it in the mail at once.

I first invited sixty-eight of the most influential Christian leaders in America and Canada to serve with Vonette and me on an invitation committee.[2] Of that number, all said they would serve except for five, each one of whom had very good reasons for not serving on the committee.

The number on the committee eventually grew to seventy-three, and their enthusiasm for a united time of fasting and prayer confirmed once again that the Holy Spirit was the author and implementor of this idea. Several indicated that God also had been speaking to them about the importance of fasting.

Next I drafted a letter to other Christian leaders, inviting them to join us in Orlando, December 5–7, 1994. The letterhead read, "A Special Call to Prayer and Fasting for America." I knew that many of them could not come, for various reasons, but I prayed that at least what Adrian called "Gideon's 300" would respond favorably. I was confident that as we met together, the Holy Spirit would visit us as we fasted and prayed; and that they would return to their radio and television programs, to their pulpits, and to various publications to spread the news of this fresh call of God to revival for America. God moved far beyond my expectations as more than six hundred came to fast and pray.

Buoyed by the remarkable response of so many Christian leaders, I sensed God leading me to write a book to further accelerate the coming revival. Because of my own experience of fasting without adequate medical counsel and because there are so few good books on spiritual fasting, I felt this book was greatly needed.

Others Join in Fasting

All during my long days without solid food, I put no pressure on Vonette—or any of my associates—to fast with me.

"The Lord has called me to fast," I explained. "Please don't fast just because I am fasting, unless God leads you."

Several of my associates did fast a few days. Five were led of the Lord to fast a full forty days—my beloved colleague Dr. Ben Jennings, Campus Crusade's international prayer coordinator; Gwyn Marolis, my office manager; Jerry Weaver, research and development coordinator for the JESUS Video Saturation Project; Mike Burns, our international liaison for staff opportunities; and Al Stahl, our World Intercessory Network coordinator.

Vonette shares a prominent part in this story. She prayed for me as she went about her responsibilities. Her particular interest—and Campus Crusade ministry—is to direct Women Today International, a movement to enlist millions of women to help fulfill the Great Commission. Two weeks before the end of my fast, she felt led of the Lord to join me.

I can't tell you what that meant to me. We have had a wonderful God-blessed marriage since our wedding in 1948, but her decision to fast on this occasion brought us together in an even more meaningful way. We drank our water and fruit juices, seeking His face as a couple, listening to what He might be saying to either of us.

Fast Celebration With Staff

On the thirty-ninth day of my fast, on a Friday afternoon, Vonette and I met with several hundred members of our Campus Crusade headquarters staff for a "Fast Celebration," to tell them our story. News about what God was saying to us had already spread throughout our headquarters, and we wanted them to hear the account directly from us. The staff had been very supportive, writing notes, speaking daily encouragements, and praying for the Lord to strengthen us.

The auditorium was packed. Our people were standing against walls and in doorways. There was a stir, and you could hear the buzz of excited talk from the crowd.

Our executive vice president, Dr. Steve Douglass, who had fasted one meal each day for forty days, introduced Vonette. The audience waited with anticipation as she stepped to the podium. "I heard some of you asking, 'Is Vonette fasting? What is Vonette going to do?'" she began. "I think you thought I was going to miss out on something special from God. And frankly, I was thinking about that too."

I felt warmed by her next words. "I really joined the fast to support my husband, to join him with one heart. But if God was going to give any special messages, I most assuredly wanted to be in on it."

When the laughter subsided, she continued. "I wasn't sure what God was going to give me, but there was an assurance that my husband is my spiritual leader, and that I can follow him." Then glancing at me, she added, "The Holy Spirit assured me that He called Bill to fast forty days, and that I could trust him in it." Many nodded their approval as Vonette continued:

"This morning in my regular devotional reading, I came across Isaiah 58 where it says God will allow us to be the repairer of the broken walls of this nation. I believe one of the reasons God has called us to fast is so we will meet His conditions, so He *can* use us..."

Then Vonette, in her thirteenth day of fasting, broke in humility before the huge crowd. Struggling through her tears, she managed to say to these intent listeners, "I believe He is calling us to fast...so He can use us to be a part of this spiritual awakening...in this country...throughout the world." Suddenly, she could say no more. Quickly turning, she left the podium.

The hundreds of staff rose to their feet with a burst of applause. Later, reflecting on the day, some would say that the staff's love for Vonette caused a lump to rise in every throat and tears to moisten every eye.

As the applause died down, I followed her at the podium. "I believe God wants to do something new in all of our lives," I began. "I believe He has something special for each one of us. Over the years, God has given Campus Crusade the privilege of helping to take the gospel to at least 1.5 billion people, and tens of millions have indicated salvation decisions for Christ. To God be all the praise and glory.

"But even in this ministry, we—like the church at Ephesus—can leave our first love. We, too, can experience a slow kind of spiritual erosion. So I am impressed to ask you: Are you really experiencing a vital, personal, intimate walk with our Lord Jesus Christ? Is there anything hindering you in your walk? Are you all that God wants you to be? Is there something that you need to confess to the Lord?" Then I quoted Romans 12:1,2:

> I beseech you therefore, brethren, by the mercies of God, that you present your bodies a living sacrifice, holy, acceptable to God, which is your reasonable service. And do not be conformed to this world, but be transformed by the renewing of your mind, that you may prove what is that good and acceptable and perfect will of God (NKJ).

"The important thing to remember," I continued, "is that our remaining time here on earth is very short. The Lord may come soon, or He may challenge us to do more for Him than we are now doing. But in terms of eternity, none of us is going to live very long. Some of you may be here another fifty years, but such time is still relatively short."

I searched the hushed crowd with my eyes. The staff seemed focused on my every word. "Our nation needs revival," I said. "And I believe that revival needs to start with us. It needs to start right here in this room. I don't want to appeal to just your emotions, but I do want to appeal to your will. Come join me and say, 'Oh Spirit of God, breathe on me...touch me...give me a new and vital and more dynamic relationship with You.' If that is your desire, will you come forward?"

Without another word, hundreds came forward to kneel and pray. Their love for Christ had prompted them to join staff in the first place. Now they were demonstrating their desire to continue in their ministry with pure hearts, free of sin, filled with the Holy Spirit. The response was unanimous.

Our Great Resource

America is a great resource providing more money, technology, and manpower to help fulfill the Great Commission than all other countries combined. If the enemies of the gospel had their way, America would no longer be a great sending nation; Satan would take away all of our religious freedoms.

God does not tolerate sin. The Bible and history make this painfully clear. I believe God has given ancient Israel as an example of what will happen to the United States if we do not experience revival. He will continue to discipline us with all kinds of problems until we repent or until we are destroyed, as was ancient Israel because of her sin of disobedience.

The Lord sent all sorts of calamities upon Israel, trying to get her attention and cause her to repent:

> "And still you won't return to me," says the Lord. "Therefore I will bring upon you all these further evils I have spoken of. Prepare to meet your God in judgment, Israel. For you are dealing with the one who formed the mountains and made the winds, and knows your every thought…Jehovah, the Lord, the Lord Almighty, is his name" (Amos 4:11–13, TLB).

This idea is reinforced with terrible warning in Deuteronomy 28:58–62:

> If you refuse to obey…refusing reverence to the glorious and fearful name of Jehovah your God, then Jehovah will send perpetual plagues upon you and upon your children…The Lord will bring upon you every sickness and plague there is, even those not mentioned in this book, until you are destroyed. There will be few of you left, though before you were as numerous as stars. All this if you do not listen to the Lord your God (TLB).

God is calling the Church to rise up and lead the nation to repent and follow Him. Our only hope is a supernatural visit from God.

CHAPTER 3

America Under Judgment

Amerca has a unique relationship with God. Beginning with Christopher Columbus, the pilgrims, the Founding Fathers, Christian homes, schools, and other institutions, no other nation in history has been so blessed of God. As we salute the flag, we pledge allegiance to "one nation, under God, indivisible, with liberty and justice for all." Our national motto is "In God We Trust."

We have received blessing upon blessing from the hand of God. Our 250 million people represent only 6 percent of the world's population, but we boast 54 percent of the world's wealth. We have opened our hearts to the poor and helped feed the hungry of the world. In times of emergency, we have given generously even to our enemies. As for ourselves, our "needs" often are "wants," and most of us never lack the necessities of life.

A Nation Without Soul

But over the years, America has gone astray. We live in a nation that has lost its soul. Our abundance has led to greed. Our freedom has become license to turn away from God and pursue the role of the prodigal. Our national religious heritage is being forgotten or ridiculed as irrelevant or old fashioned.

America has become one of the most sinful nations in the world. We have done more to destroy the morality of other countries than any nation in history. We have become the single greatest market on the globe for illegal drugs, and we lead the world in exporting pornographic magazines and films.

Let us take a close look at a few of the compelling evidences of America's lost condition.

First, *the secularization of public life.* Our people find themselves "free" to remove God, the Bible, and prayer from the classroom and the workplace; to demand the removal of holiday religious symbols from public places; and to persecute Christians who insist on honoring God where they work and play.

What happened to singer Smokey Robinson in Sarasota, Florida, is a good example of this secularization. Smokey was a scheduled speaker for a two-day Youth Explosion Anti-Drug rally. On the first day, he testified how God had rescued him from drug abuse. As a result, his speech for the second day was canceled.

"I talked to them about loving each other," Smokey said. "I told them they had to change all the hand-me-down prejudice they were living under...But when I started to talk to them about what God has done in my life, I stepped on some toes.

"The killing thing," he said, "is that you can go into schools, talk about the Charles Manson murders and tell all the gory details, describe sexual promiscuity and pass out condoms, and talk about Hitler. But if you mention God or Jesus, it's taboo. Now that's a shame."[1]

William J. Bennett, who served as secretary of education under President Reagan, says:

> The problem isn't that public schools don't teach that Jesus Christ is the Lord; they shouldn't do that, and they are constitutionally prohibited from doing that. What the American people don't understand, and I think they are right not to understand it, is that a group of students can, [by] law, get together and say, "We must all advance the Marxist revolution."

In too many places in American public education, religion has been ignored, banned, or shunned in ways that serve neither knowledge, nor the Constitution, nor sound public policy. There is no good curricular or constitutional reason for textbooks to ignore, as many do, the role of religion in the founding of this country or its prominent place in the lives of many of its citizens. We should acknowledge that religion—from the Pilgrims to the civil rights struggle—is an important part of our history, civics, literature, art, music, poetry, and politics, and we should insist that our schools tell the truth about it.[2]

Bennett's support of voluntary prayers and the posting of the Ten Commandments in our public schools was characterized as an invitation to "Khomeinism and Kahaneism."[3]

As a result of secularism, our nation has descended into the pits. Columnist Cal Thomas writes:

We have abandoned an objective standard for right and wrong. Beginning with the assault on prayer and Bible reading in public schools, various activist groups have removed virtually all standards for objective truth. They replaced them with secularism, pluralism, and a revulsion for imposing anything on anybody, under a misguided notion that the Constitution forbids it.

Thirty years of inattention to character, virtue, morality, and a definition of right and wrong has led us to the present. A nation that has focused on physical fitness and changing the oil in our increasingly expensive cars every 3,000 miles has ignored the societal "manual" that requires certain moral and spiritual "additives" if we are to enjoy an orderly society.[4]

Second, *our so-called "social problems."* Crime and violence among our youth, race riots, rape, divorce, sexual promiscuity, teen pregnancy, abortion, AIDS, and drug and alcohol addiction have become epidemics. Like a cresting tidal wave, they threaten to sweep away every decent vestige left in our society. As a result, Americans are experiencing a deepening sense of powerlessness and pessimism over the future of our country.

Crime has emerged as America's overwhelming concern. Children, who are our future, are fast becoming our greatest fear. More and more violence is invading our schools. And it is not just a problem in our inner cities, says Dr. Bernard Z. Friedlander, a professor of psychology at the University of Hartford. "It's an American problem."[5]

Child-on-child brutality on and off campus frequently makes the news. The National Association of School Psychologists reported that one in seven U.S. school children is either bullied or a bully.[6] One wonders how children can become so cold-hearted as in a recent case of two ten-year-olds in Chicago who pushed a five-year-old boy to his death simply because he refused to steal candy for them.

Attacks on teachers by students are becoming commonplace. According to the school psychologists' report, more than five thousand secondary-school teachers are physically attacked every month.[7] Little wonder. Children have lost all respect for their elders, and teachers are virtually powerless to discipline their students.

Weapons have become an alarming menace on the campus. More and more young people all over the country are carrying them to school—some for protection because gang and drug cultures are spreading rampantly, but many because they think violence is a way to settle their differences.[8] The University of Michigan recently surveyed the effects of weapons among U.S. eighth graders. The study revealed:

> Nineteen percent have been threatened with a weapon in school, and 9 percent have been injured. Forty-four percent have had property stolen, while 34 percent report having property vandalized.[9]

In an article in *Woman's Day,* writer Kathryn Stechert Black cites several chilling facts about this problem:

- According to the National Crime Survey, almost three million crimes occur on or near school campuses every year.
- Two-thirds of school administrators predict an increase in school violence.
- Nearly one in five high-school students carries a weapon; one in twenty has a gun.[10]

"Crime in general, and crime by the youngest in particular," writes *News York Times* reporter Celia W. Dugger, "has become a national obsession. The arrest rate for juveniles for murder has climbed 60 percent in a decade, according to the Federal Bureau of Investigation."[11]

Chuck Colson, chairman of Prison Fellowship Ministries in Washington, D.C., says, "The moral collapse in America is so overwhelming that it is causing an institutional crisis. We can't build prisons fast enough to take these kids off the street who are committing remorseless, consciousless crimes. Unless we deal with the moral roots of the problem, it will destroy us.

"There are 1,014,000 people in prison in America," he says. "That's a 400 percent increase in the last twenty years. During the same period, violent crime has gone up 550 percent. The moral breakdown of our society is so overwhelming, with a million more teenagers coming into the population in the next four years. A million more! And that's where most of the violent crime is being committed."[12] Colson suggests that unless the situation changes, people may be willing to surrender their liberties just to get order.

Third, *disintegration of the traditional family.* Unhappy, broken homes are a prominent part of American life. The Carnegie Corporation of New York—led by a panel of eminent politicians, doctors, educators, and business executives—paints a bleak picture of disintegrating families, persistent poverty, and high levels of child abuse.[13]

The cover story of *Time* magazine recently reported that fathers in record numbers are either abandoning or neglecting their children. Reporter Nancy Gibbs writes, "More children will go to sleep tonight in a fatherless home than ever in the nation's history."[14] Quick and easy divorce contributes significantly to this phenomenon. Armand M. Nicholi Jr., author and associate clinical professor of psychiatry at Harvard University, writes:

> The divorce rate has risen 700 percent in this century and continues to rise. There is now one divorce for every 1.8 marriages. Over a million children a year are involved in divorce cases and 13 million children under eighteen have one or both parents missing.[15]

Nicholi cites several other alarming factors in the disintegration of the family:

- Overworked working mothers, especially those with young children. This has increased marital stress and contributed to the high divorce rate.

- The notion that the traditional role of wife and mother is passé.

- Too much television: The average viewing time for children is twenty to twenty-four hours per week.

- Uncontrolled aggression in the home, resulting in an alarming increase in child battering.

- A change in childrearing because of promiscuity, perversion, and the shift of child care from the home to outside agencies.

- Parental resentment of children because they interfere with their parents' fulfillment.

"In our day we are seeing an all-out assault on the family," Nicholi says. "It is coming from many different sources. We must become aware of these sources so that we can wisely build a spiritual 'wall of protection' around the family as a strong base to turn our nation back to God."[16]

The disintegration of the family is largely to blame for the phenomenal rise in crime among our youth. "Studies of young criminals," writes Gibbs, "have found that more than 70 percent of all juveniles in state reform institutions come from fatherless homes."[17]

Fourth, *a spirit of selfishness*, which seems to have gripped much of our nation. The biblical imperatives to "love your neighbor as yourself" (Luke 27:10) and "do to others what you would have them do to you" (Matthew 7:12) have largely fallen prey to a "me-first" and "do to others before they do it to you" mentality. Again we turn to our youth to view the reflection of our national neglect. Allan Bloom, a professor of social thought at the University of Chicago, writes:

> Students are free of most constraints, and their families make sacrifices for them without asking for much in the way of obedience or respect. Religion and national origin have almost no noticeable effect on their social life or their career prospects...Their primary preoccupation is themselves, understood in the narrowest sense.[18]

More than two hundred years ago, Jean Jacques Rousseau saw with alarm the seeds of the breakdown of the family. Addressing this issue, he found that the critical connection between man and woman was being broken by individualism. Today, Bloom says "Everyone has 'his own little separate system'...and the aptest description of the state of students' souls is the psychology of separateness."[19] He goes on to assert, "The most visible sign of our increasing separateness and, in turn, the cause of ever greater separateness is divorce."[20]

Even Christians have fallen into the "me-first" trap. Many have forsaken integrity for selfish gain. Divorce, the cause of increasing separateness, is almost as common among

Christians as it is in society. Churches across the land experience the same difficulties as other entities as they appeal for individuals to make commitments. Nevertheless, "selfishness in this case is not in itself a moral vice or sin but a natural necessity. The 'me generation' and 'narcissism' are merely descriptions, not causes."[21]

Professor David Larsen relates that, in sharp contrast to the individualism of modern secular society, "every description of the church used in the New Testament emphasizes the interrelatedness of believers in Christ. As the Body of Christ, the church consists of many diverse parts working together in extraordinary harmony and efficiency." Larsen argues that "our experience of genuine spiritual community is deficient" due in part to an exaggerated individualism in Western culture. "Any believer who pretends to be the Lone Ranger is not facing reality. Believers need each other in the spiritual battle in which they engage…Scripture insists that we are bound together in the bundle of life and that our interdependency as believers bears significantly on the renewing of our minds."[22]

Fifth, *decisions of the Supreme Court.* Rulings by justices during the 1940s and 1960s brought government into direct contact with religious life in the United States.

In *Everson v. Board of Education* (1947), the Court sharply defined "the separation of church and state." In effect, the majority of justices—in contradiction to the beliefs of our Founding Fathers—misinterpreted the Constitution. They said that the basic document guaranteeing our freedom requires us to keep God out of government and public life. That decision made it easier for those seeking to remove the influence of Christian faith from schools and other public sectors.

Often the Court's decisions reflect the condition of our culture. Although the 1947 ruling contributed significantly to the decadence of our country, the seeds of this disintegration were sown earlier by secular humanists.

In *Engel v. Vitale* (1962), the Supreme Court banned state-directed prayers in public schools, and in *Abington School District v. Schempp* (1963), the Court ruled against Bible reading for religious purposes in public schools. Justices later affirmed the propriety of studying the Bible and other religious texts as literature, but not as a religious observance required of all children.[23]

Most school officials have zealously followed this rule. Some, however, have joined the many students, parents, and community and religious leaders across the country to resist the Court's decisions. Recently, for example, the principal of a high school in Jackson, Mississippi, granted the request of a number of his students when they asked to recite the following prayer over the school's public address system:

> Almighty God, we ask that You bless our parents, teachers, and country throughout the day. In Your name, we pray. Amen.[24]

Although the prayer was initiated by the students, a legally allowed practice, the principal was fired. In protest, more than four thousand people of all religious affiliations converged on the grounds of the Capitol in Jackson to support the principal.[25]

In 1973, the *Roe v. Wade* decision made it legal to slaughter unborn babies in the womb. By 1994, more than thirty million had been murdered—burned to death with saline solutions or torn limb from limb by cold steel forceps in the hands of ruthless, morally bankrupt doctors.

In 1980, the Court said schools could no longer post the Ten Commandments.[26] Classifying them as "plainly religious," the ruling held that the Ten Commandments might prompt children to read, ponder, revere, or obey the commandments.

Bennett calls the extremes to which some go to deny religion its place in American life "mind-boggling." As of this writing, for example, a case is pending in Federal Court that could ban the Ten Commandments even from our courtrooms.

For years Richard Suhre, an 84-year-old North Carolina atheist, had objected to a tablet display of the Ten Commandments behind a judge's bench in the main courtroom of the Haywood County Courthouse. Filing suit to have the tablets removed, he charged that the display violates the Constitution's First Amendment clause guaranteeing freedom of religion.

"I am very tired of being dictated to by the pious," Suhre said. "For several years, I have been objecting to the biblical writing on the walls of the courthouse. First, because it's an advertisement for the church on public property. Second, because the Jesus freaks on the jury will read the laws of Moses and make their decisions on the laws of Moses instead of the laws of North Carolina."

Although more than 16,000 citizens signed a petition to save the tablets, the atheist vowed to continue fighting for "his right for his government to be religion-free."

According to the *Charlotte Observer*, the atheist said making his fellow citizens uncomfortable is tonic. "I can laugh at the whole thing," Suhre said. "If I were inclined to worry about it all, I'd be sick."[27]

Sixth, *the homosexual "explosion."* According to pollster George Barna of the Barna Research Group, homosexuals are a small group by percentage in our country. "Most evidence," he says, "indicates that somewhere between 1 and 3 percent of the adult population engages in homosexual contact with some level of frequency, and that less than 1 percent might be deemed exclusively homosexual."[28] But despite their relatively few numbers, militant homosexuality has exploded onto the American scene, abetted by network media.

Arrogantly demanding their "rights," activist gays and lesbians have become a militant voice in American politics, influencing elections and affecting the policies of high

government leaders. Their public demonstrations and political lobbying have fooled many in our country into believing that they deserve special status.

Secular humanists and other anti-Christian forces in our
land who embrace homosexuals as a minority are fighting
to protect them with special laws. If they succeed, one
cannot help but ponder the potential impact of these laws
on the hiring practices of religious organizations.

The first chapter of the Book of Romans clearly shows
that God has cursed those who insist on practicing and
promoting homosexuality:

> God gave them over to shameful lusts. Even their
> women exchanged natural relations for unnatural
> ones. In the same way the men also abandoned natural
> relations with women and were inflamed with lust for
> one another. Men committed indecent acts with other
> men, and received in themselves the due penalty for
> their perversion (Romans 1:26,27).

And in Leviticus 20:13, God says:

> If a man lies with a man as one lies with a woman,
> both of them have done what is detestable.

Romans chapter one makes it plain that we can say the
same about lesbians.

Although God has clearly expressed His displeasure of
the homosexual lifestyle, His Word assures us that He loves
the homosexual person as much as He does the most dedicated, spiritually mature Christian. We are commanded to
follow His example and love the sinner while rejecting their
sinful lifestyle. This also applies to other individuals and
their sinful actions that grieve the heart of God.

Although homosexuals are small in number, their far-
reaching influence upon society is cause for alarm. Our love
for the sinner must not weaken our rejection of the sin.
That much of our society seems to have lost its once-high

moral resolve is further evidence of America's slide into decadence.

Our Nation's Survival

It is sobering to realize that we are no longer "one nation under God." And, unless America turns back to Him as a people, there is no way our country can survive.

God destroyed the wicked cities of Sodom and Gomorrah (Genesis 19:1–29). In A.D. 70, God judged His people, the Jews, sending the Roman army down upon them. The soldiers leveled Jerusalem, killing thousands of people. The Jewish remnant then scattered among the nations and have suffered severe persecution ever since.

> *"The Church has to come together on its knees. The people of God must repent and seek God's will because the battle is a spiritual battle."*
>
> —*Chuck Colson, chairman*
> *Prison Fellowship Ministries*
> *Washington, D.C.*

Rome was the mightiest empire in the history of the world. But it decayed morally until civil disobedience broke out on a massive scale. Rome became so weak that she fell prey to uprisings within and to the barbarian hoards without.

These are warnings that God will not tolerate sin. Throughout Scripture, God has made His message clear: "If you obey Me, I will bless you. If you disobey Me, I will discipline you. And if you continue to disobey Me, I will destroy you."

In 2 Chronicles 28:5–8, we see that God judged Judah. The kings of Syria and Israel killed Judah's men and carried off her women and children.

That is awesome judgment. God often uses a nation or nations to punish those who continue in sin. World War II is a good example, when the Allies defeated enemy forces.

God also uses nature to carry out His judgments. Ancient Egypt suffered pollution of the Nile, hordes of frogs, an infestation of lice, swarms of flies and locusts, a deadly plague upon their livestock, an epidemic of boils, a severe hail and lightning storm, and ultimately the death of the first-born sons of Egyptians. The disasters left Egypt in ruins and families devastated with sorrow (Exodus 7:15—11:6). I believe God may be trying to get our attention through the avalanche of "natural" disasters that have come upon us—fires, floods, hurricanes, tornados, and earthquakes.

America is sowing in shame and reaping in judgment. The Bible says, "They sow the wind and reap the whirlwind" (Hosea 8:7). Under the judgment of God, we are reaping what we have sown.

Where Do We Turn?

We face crisis after crisis and, from the human perspective, there is no hope. So the question naturally arises, where do we turn for help?

How about the Supreme Court? The justices used to be the most revered, honored persons in our country. When I was growing up, I considered every member of the Court to be just a little below sainthood. But the decisions of some of the justices have led the nation away from the traditional biblical values of our Founding Fathers and brought the curses of God upon our land. In conflict with our Constitution, the justices often have usurped the legislative process and made decisions that only Congress is authorized to make.

How about education? We know that Germany and Japan are the most literate nations in the world. But they were the ones largely responsible for World War II. The depraved conduct of the Germans and Japanese in time of war was indescribable.

In America, influential educators have taken God out of our textbooks. They teach evolution and deny the biblical view of creation. Moral relativism is destroying our young people. Advising them to do "whatever feels good," these educators deny God's authority by contending that values are relative to the individual and the situation.

How about government? It has become increasingly corrupt, and our nation is well aware of it. While our $3 trillion national debt threatens to bankrupt the country, Congress steadfastly refuses to take appropriate action. Legislators fall prey to pork barrel projects for the folks back home, and to well-healed lobbyists bent on promoting programs for their clients. Voters no longer trust their representatives. The people know the country is in serious trouble, and they blame Washington for it. In the words of Chuck Colson, "You cannot change by political means what is a deep-rooted moral and cultural malaise."

How about business and professional people? Today, you can hardly trust anyone, even in the Christian community. How often have you heard, "Never do business with a Christian"? Moral standards are at an all-time low. A handshake, a promise, a pledge, a contract—these mean very little anymore. Businessmen and professionals are seen as selfish, greedy people who may "rip you off" unless you are careful.

How about the media? With few restrictions, except a call to be responsible, the press has enjoyed a freedom unparalleled in other countries. But the press, now called the media because of radio and television, has relinquished its once lofty ideals. Sensationalism has replaced solid, responsible reporting. Today, the media captures our attention with blood, violence, and sex. Of course, if you challenge them, their leaders will say, "That's what the people want." Or, "Don't try to force your Christian values on us. We have constitutional rights."

How about the Church? It is part of the problem. The masses are crying for help, but they are not turning to God's people.

Why?

"The Church is often running off in different direc-
tions," Colson says, "and it's almost as competitive as the
political world." Thanks to ministers caught in sexual sins
and the divorce court; flamboyant preachers in expensive
attire badgering the public for money; the lax moral climate
in our congregations; and the media's incessant portrayal
of ministers as sissies, buffoons, and con artists, unbelievers
have concluded that Christians are no different than the
rest of society.

So here we are, living in the most critical moment in the
history of America, a period I view as being far more crucial
than any time since the War of Independence from Great
Britain. It is far more perilous than the dangerous days of
the Civil War. And I think, from the human perspective,
there is no way that our nation can survive. There is no place
to turn now—except to God.

CHAPTER 4

The Impotent Church

ost Christians in America have lost their sense of a
holy God. They do not understand His divine attributes of love, power, wisdom, sovereignty, and grace.
Vast numbers of church members do not know that He is
present, active, available, and knowable to them. According
to numerous surveys, 50 percent of the hundred million who
attend church each Sunday have no assurance of their
salvation. And 95 percent are not familiar with the person
and ministry of the Holy Spirit. Only two percent of believers
in America regularly share their faith in Christ with others.

The reality of God seems far removed from everyday life.
As a result, it has become all too easy to be influenced by the
incessant onslaught of secular attitudes in movies, television, advertising, and daily peer pressure.

For a great many Christians, God is a mental concept to
consider on Sunday morning. Indeed, the chief sin in the
Church today is unbelief. It is impossible to be "on fire" for
God when He is not real to you.

George Barna, who regularly conducts polls to take the
Christian pulse in America, offers an alarming report.

He writes that observers in England believe America is
undergoing a devastating spiritual change similar to what
happened there in recent times. These observers "recall
when England was a nation in which the Church was the
central institution in society. Moral values, social behavior,
cultural activities, family development, lifestyles, and even
political decision-making all revolved around the nation's

religious perspective and spiritual sensitivity. Ingrained in the nation's thinking was the belief that the highest goal in life is to worship and serve God." Barna continues:

> More recently [in England] these values have been undermined by the encroachment of secularism. There is more concern now for the material than for the spiritual. God is no longer at the center of the nation's agenda. Its Christian community has all but disappeared. Once representing the vast majority of that great nation's population, true believers are estimated now to be only about two percent of the population.
>
> There are striking similarities between the spiritual decline of England and the current spiritual condition of the United States. A thoughtful evaluation of modern America—our social, political, spiritual, moral, and economic condition—shows how insidiously our own spiritual foundations are deteriorating. We, too, are a materialistic society, more concerned about the physical comforts of today than the spiritual needs of the future. It is very hard to persuade us to think seriously about the effects of cultural change on the nation's religious beliefs and behavior.
>
> The result is that the Christian community, in the midst of a whirlpool of change and a hostile societal environment, is losing the battle...Consequently, America in the '90s is rotting from the inside out...Service to God has been replaced by a thirst for exaltation of self.[1]

Importance of the Local Church

The most important and influential institution for the good of mankind in any community is the church of our Lord Jesus Christ. But many have fallen away from her.

For example, sometime ago on a flight to Chicago, I was witnessing to a fellow passenger. When I asked if he were a Christian, he casually and flippantly said that he wasn't very religious. He was forced to attend church as a boy and vowed that when he left home, he would never attend again. He made it clear to me that the church had nothing to offer him.

I asked him if he would like to live in a community where there were no churches. He looked at me a bit startled and exclaimed, "Of course not!"

"Did it ever occur to you that you are a parasite?" I asked.

"What do you mean by that?" he demanded.

"Well, you want all the benefits of the church in your community, but you are not willing to contribute anything," I explained.

He sat silently for a moment, then responded enthusiastically. "I'll be in church on Sunday."

Many like to attend church services because it makes them feel good, but they do not want to get involved in the work of the Lord. That is what they pay the pastor to do —visit newcomers, counsel, provide an exciting youth program, and, for the one thousandth time, preach something encouraging from the Twenty-Third Psalm.

In my almost fifty years of walking with the Lord, I have been committed to the local church. My wife and I became Christians through the influence of the First Presbyterian Church of Hollywood, where we were nourished in our faith as young believers.

Shortly after receiving Christ, while continuing my business interests in Hollywood, I began graduate study at Princeton Theological Seminary and later transferred to Fuller Theological Seminary to be closer to my business. I continued my studies for five years while also serving as a deacon in the church and chairman of a large evangelistic team. More than a hundred workers were involved in a very active witnessing program.

In 1951, God gave me the vision to help take the gospel of Christ to the world. That vision became Campus Crusade for Christ, also currently called *NewLife2000*. From the beginning, Vonette and I have viewed the local church as the most vital part of the work that God is doing in the world. As a policy, each Campus Crusade staff member is required to be actively involved in a local congregation.

So strong is our commitment to the local church that approximately forty years ago, I dedicated a page in the *Four Spiritual Laws* evangelistic booklet to teaching new converts the importance of the church.[2] That message is proclaimed in the more than 1.5 billion copies of the *Four Spiritual Laws* that have been printed and distributed around the world in all major languages.

A Growing Concern

Our Lord looks upon His Church, His body of believers, as the "salt of the earth" (Matthew 5:13). Salt is a necessary supplement in the human diet. It adds flavor to the food, and as a preservative, it prolongs the life of perishable items. But most Christians today have lost their savor. And as many of the values that Americans hold dear slowly slip away, the Church often seems powerless to preserve them.

In talking with many prominent Christian leaders across our land, I have witnessed a growing concern for the tragic condition of America and the Church. It is obvious that the Holy Spirit has been at work among those who still listen to His voice, and in advance of the coming revival, He is creating this concern in the minds and hearts of His people.

Evidence of this is the enthusiastic response I received from the more than six hundred Christian leaders who attended our fasting and prayer conference in Orlando.

The Role of the Holy Spirit

The Holy Spirit, who has touched these leaders, is the author of revival. Ultimately, no Christian is going to fast and pray for a spiritual awakening unless the Spirit calls him.

Jesus said, "No one can come to me unless the Father who sent me draws him" (John 6:44). But it is the Holy

Spirit who convicts of sin: "When he comes, he will convict the world of guilt in regard to sin and righteousness and judgment... he will guide you into all truth" (John 16:8,13).

I believe that preceding the coming revival, the Holy Spirit will create in the hearts and minds of millions of believers the desire to repent, fast, and pray.

During revival, the Holy Spirit persuades believers of their true condition and their need to repent and return to their first love. He inspires His servants to speak His fresh messages to the Church. And He uses those whom He inspires to help convince other believers of their need to drop their worldly pursuits and seek after God with all their hearts.

Erosion of Spiritual Values

But if the Holy Spirit is the author of revival, how did so much of Christ's Church become so impotent?

The answer is simple: We are not listening to God. We are not obeying Him.

Over a long period of time, much of the Church has fallen away from the reality of God, and spiritually we have become like the frog in the pot.

Perhaps you have heard that story. You set a frog in a pot of water and turn the burner to its lowest setting. The water heats up ever so slowly. The frog just sets there—in the comfort of the ever-warming water—until, before he knows it, his life is cooked out of him.

That is what has happened to the Church. Over time, a slow erosion of spiritual values has taken its tragic toll.

During the last thirty years, America's slow slide into moral decadence has happened in full view of the Body of Christ. A look at conditions in the Church—and surrounding it—will help to understand why.

First, *Christians have left their first love.* According to many polls, the majority of believers have lost their original spiritual fervor and are caught up in the things of the world.

Like the Church of Ephesus (Revelation 2:1–7), they do not love the Lord as they once did.

Second, *Christians, for the most part, are sorely divided.* With far too many denominations, each with its own distinctive beliefs, the Church seems embattled over doctrinal issues, the ordination of women, abortion, and other moral principles. The ordination of homosexuals and the acceptance of gay and lesbian lifestyles, for example, have pitted some within mainline denominations against each other over the orthodox view that homosexuality is an abomination (Leviticus 18:22 and Romans 1).

> *"If people could see the unity of the Body of Christ, they would come knocking our doors down. We wouldn't be able to build churches fast enough."*
>
> —Chuck Colson, chairman
> Prison Fellowship Ministries
> Washington, D.C.

Furthermore, many congregations are torn by internal strife. Instead of being havens of rest for the spiritually weary, often churches are battle zones for the spiritually carnal. "I know as a pastor," says Steve Gould of Crystal Evangelical Free Church in Minneapolis, "that there are thousands of churches across this nation that are broken by bitterness, broken by divisiveness, broken by competitiveness, and broken by animosities between members of congregations. God is not pleased with that, and He wants to lift the spiritual darkness from those churches."

Third, *Christians often reflect a poor image.* When I was a young man, many unbelievers like myself thought the local church was a place for sissies, women, and children. Today, the independent male—in the macho image of Clint Eastwood, Harrison Ford, and Arnold Schwarzenegger—still thinks the same. Hollywood and the media have furthered that image by portraying "parsons" as weak, effeminate individuals whom "real men" find disgusting.

Hollywood often portrays ministers as men who serve God but struggle with lust for women. Unfortunately, in recent years, a number of ministers in our nation have been exposed for sexual and financial misconduct. It is estimated that 10 to 15 percent of clergy, as well as those in other helping professions, experience problems in these areas.

From the pulpit, some Christian leaders condemn sin, but privately are themselves guilty. Add to that the divorce rate among Christians, and you confirm the perception that believers are little different from nonbelievers.

The popular statistic thrown about by journalists, social scientists, and pastors for the current Christian divorce rate is 50 percent—approximately the same as that in the secular world. But according to George Barna, this is a misleading figure.

"In 1990, there were forty-eight divorces for each one hundred marriages," he says, which comes to about 1.1 million divorce cases. But the people who get divorced and who get married in any given year are not the same.[3] In other words, the people who were married in 1990 were not necessarily the ones who were divorced that year.

Over the long haul, Barna says: "Our research shows that about one-quarter of all adults who marry eventually become divorced."

In the short term, however, we're still looking at that 48 to 50 percentage rate, and Barna indicates in his "America 2000" forecast that divorce and multiple marriages will become even more acceptable in our society.[4] Things are not getting better, and many Christian leaders now view divorce as the modern-day curse of the Church.

Although precise divorce statistics among Christians are not readily available, we can easily see that the Christian divorce rate reflects that of secular society.

Why?

- We have departed from the ways of the Lord. We no longer obey God's Word on this subject.

- "No-fault" divorce has created painless litigation, making divorce an easy solution to personal difficulties in marriage.

- The stigma of divorce in the Church, as in society, has all but disappeared.

- Society and much of the Church now accept divorce as something to be expected.

- Society and the Church have failed to instill the idea that marriage is a permanent commitment.

The fact that divorce is an emotional trauma equivalent to a bout with cancer seems to escape those who want to be "liberated" from marriage circumstances.[5]

While the need to minister to hurting divorcees and their children has reached crisis proportions, this fact remains: peer pressure and church pressure *not* to divorce have been lost, and the floodgates are open. Going into marriage, divorce has become an option to almost every couple headed for the altar.

We cannot begin to calculate the effect of divorced parents on the children and on society as a whole. In the years to come, we will see the results of this acute rejection in millions of young adults whose damaged ability to trust, love, and commit to personal relationships will doom their marriages from the start.

Fourth, *Christians have lost their influence on society.* Some years ago, a major secular poll reported that there were sixty million born-again Christians in America. But publications such as the *Wall Street Journal* took issue with the finding. The *Journal* wanted to know: If this is true, why is America ravaged by crime and violence? Are not Christians supposed to be "salt and light"? If so, where is their mighty Christian influence in our bankrupt society?

The answer lies partly in the fact that millions who call themselves Christians are really not Christians at all; although religious, they have never experienced a personal relationship with Jesus Christ. And many of those who *are* Christians are living worldly (carnal) lives. The apostle John wrote:

> How can we be sure that we belong to him? By looking within ourselves: are we really trying to do what he wants us to?
>
> Someone may say, "I am a Christian; I am on my way to heaven; I belong to Christ." But if he doesn't do what Christ tells him to, he is a liar. But those who do what Christ tells them to will learn to love God more and more. That is the way to know whether or not you are a Christian. Anyone who says he is a Christian should live as Christ did (1 John 2:3–6, TLB).

As I have noted, salt brings flavor to food and helps preserve perishable goods. Jesus says, "If you lose your flavor, what will happen to the world?" (Matthew 5:13, TLB). The problem with the Church today is that because many Christians have lost their savor, they are leaving a bad taste in the mouth of society. And most believers are struggling even to survive in the world, let alone preserve it.

Fifth, *Christians are searching for easy solutions and quick success.* Most of God's ministers shun fiery sermons on holiness and repentance. Instead, they pander to the desires of their flocks, preaching "feel-good" messages on health, wealth, and success in life. It seems the focus from many pulpits is on how to improve the believer's material and mental lot in life, rather than seeking first the kingdom of God and His righteousness (Matthew 6:33) and fulfilling the Great Commission (Matthew 28:18–20).

Many preachers oversell the benefits of being a Christian. And, as a result, they lead believers toward "easy believism" and the shipwreck of disillusionment with their faith. Quoting Jesus, Billy Graham writes:

He says, "My yoke is easy and my burden is light" (Matthew 11:30). Nevertheless, He calls us to follow Him, regardless of the cost, and He never promises that our path will always be smooth.[6]

Our Lord suffered the agony of the cross for us. The apostle Paul's life was filled with disappointment, pain, suffering, and eventually martyrdom, along with spiritual victories (2 Corinthians 11:22–33).

"No life is without its own set of problems," Graham says. "When I decided to give my life to Jesus Christ as a young man, it was not because I believed He would take away all my pain. No, I trusted Him because He promised me eternal life, and I believed He would always be with me and give me the strength to cope with the difficulties of this life."

> *"The Church has developed a theology that doesn't require much repentance. We have a theology that is uncomfortable with the very term 'Jesus is Lord.'"*
>
> —Dr. Paul A. Cedar, president Evangelical Free Church of America

Corrie ten Boom, a survivor of the Ravensbruk Nazi concentration camp, used to say, "The worst can happen but the *best* remains."

"That is a wonderful message," Graham says, "because we all have to endure storms in our lives. When any preacher or teacher oversells either the material or the spiritual benefits of the Christian life, I believe he is contributing to the work of the horseman (demon) who deceives. There is nothing on earth to compare with new life in Jesus Christ, but it will not always be easy…"[7]

Billy Graham also has strong words concerning preachers who warp the truth about the Christian walk by reporting only accounts of spiritual victory, thereby setting up believers for disappointment with God in their own lives:

> When we tell only the stories of victory, we tell only a part of the truth. When we recount only the answered prayers, we oversimplify. When we imply that the Christian faith involves no yoke and no burden, we tell less than the whole truth.[8]

Half-truths and easy answers to hard questions, he says, amount to nothing more than deceiving the flock. As for the Christian life and material gain, Graham continues:

> In a time of stress and uncertainty in his life, the apostle Paul wrote to the church at Philippi: "I have learned in whatever state I am, to be content: I know how to be abased, and I know how to abound. Everywhere and in all things I have learned both to be full and to be hungry, both to abound and to suffer need." And then he added these stirring words: "I can do all things through Christ who strengthens me" (Philippians 4:11–13, NKJ).[9]

Wealth and success are not the only harmful teachings tearing at the confidence of believers in America. An entire genre of self-help, do-it-yourself books has flooded the Christian market, emulating its counterpart in the secular world. It is as though the Word of God and the Spirit of God are not sufficient to cope with the problems of the '90s. So, many have turned to psychology, emphasizing the inward search, the psyche, the soul, looking for help in self-diagnosis (with a few Christian principles thrown in by writers to qualify it as Christian material).

Sixth, *the Church is weakened by a "what's-the-use?" mentality.* Many Christians, when confronted with world conditions and the call to Christian action, reply with a shrug, "Jesus said it was going to happen, so why worry about it?" Instead of becoming more motivated to help spread the gospel and share their faith with everyone who will listen, they live for the "rapture," for escape. They plunge themselves into pleasure-seeking and self-worship, waiting for the end to come.

Seventh, *the world has so crept into the Church that it has become culturally conditioned.* Findings by Barna Research led to the following conclusion:

> Charged by Christ Himself to be agents to change the world rather than agents changed by the world, we have been mesmerized by the lures of modern culture.[10]

To some extent, the Church is aware of this, but has difficulty separating itself from the immoral influences of our culture. This is easy to see in the dress and behavior of many church-goers and in the worldly entertainment they seek.

Saturated at home by what would be R-rated television, many find it easy to enjoy R-rated movies at the theater. Films soak their minds with violence, lurid sex, and profanity. Using the Lord's name in vain has become standard fare in films, just an expected part of the entertainment. Desensitized by so much of it, unoffended believers munch hot popcorn and wash it down with cold cola as they intently follow the plot.

It is apparent that most believers are burning with spiritual indifference, and have little concern for the souls of nonbelievers. But is the demise of the Church in America a foregone conclusion? Absolutely not.

Our Alternative

We do not have to be like the Ephesian Christians—having left our first love (Revelation 2:4). We do not have to be like the Laodician Christians—neither hot nor cold, but wealthy and in need of nothing, blind to the fact that we are spiritually "wretched, miserable, poor, blind, and naked," in danger of being spewed out of God's mouth (Revelation 3:15–17, NKJ).

Each one of us has the Word of God. We can read and understand and obey it. We can turn to God. We can seek Him. We do not have to wait on others to lead the way.

We can walk in the Spirit. In the power He supplies, we can refuse to be ruled by our "flesh." With the help of the Holy Spirit, we can win the struggle with our carnal nature by refusing to obey it (Galatians 5:16,17). We do not *have* to follow the ways of the world (1 John 2:1–6; 15–17).

Most of the Church in America finds itself in this present state of spiritual impotence because it does not truly love God, nor trust His promises and obey His commands. Most believers do not spend time with the Lord in prayer or study His holy Word. They do not know or appreciate His many attributes. They live with a limited view of our great Creator God, our holy heavenly Father; and our risen, incomparable, peerless Savior, the Lord Jesus Christ.

If you do not understand how holy, powerful, righteous, and loving God is, you cannot very well love and trust Him. God's Word declares that without faith it is impossible to please Him (Hebrews 11:6). The Bible says, "The righteous will live by faith" (Romans 1:17). But if you believe in a small God who is no bigger than you are, you are not going to place much faith in Him. Nor will you be motivated to love, trust, and obey Him.

I am often reminded of something I have tried to teach our Campus Crusade staff and others: All we really have to do as believers, from the time we get up in the morning until we go to bed at night, is love God with all of our heart and soul and mind and strength, obey His commands, and trust His promises. That is all. Everything else flows from that.

This is what the coming revival will be all about—calling the people of God to repentance and bringing them back to their first love, to a life of faith and joyful obedience.

CHAPTER 5

Revival Fires

A wonderful revival is sweeping over Wales. The whole country, from the city to [the mines] underground, is aflame with gospel glory..."[1]

The leader of this great spiritual awakening in 1904 was a young Welsh miner with coal dust in his hair and grime beneath his fingernails. He possessed no skills as an orator, nor was he widely read. The only book he knew was the Bible, and his heart burned with a passion for God and His holy Word.

For years, Evan Roberts yearned to preach the gospel, and he cried out daily to his heavenly Father to change him and use him. When Roberts reached twenty-five, his landlady evicted him for preaching and praying loudly in his room. Down in the mines, while friends smoked and laughed on their breaks, he sat quietly reading his Bible.

One day in 1904 while Roberts was in prayer, God revealed to him that He was going to send a revival to Wales, and that one hundred thousand unbelievers would turn to Christ. Then the Holy Spirit showed Roberts that the coming revival would spread like a prairie fire to England, then to all of Europe, Africa, and Asia.

Burning with this vision, Roberts sought opportunity to preach, but found none. He begged his pastor to let him preach, but at first the bewildered minister said no to this overly enthusiastic coal miner. Finally, after much pleading, the pastor relented.

"All right, Evan, you can preach following the Wednesday night service," he said, "if anyone chooses to stay and listen."

Seventeen curious seekers stayed behind. The young evangelist boldly proclaimed what he had heard from God. His message was simple: 1) You must confess every known sin to God; 2) you must remove every doubtful habit from your life; 3) you must obey the Holy Spirit's prompting; and 4) you must go public with your witness for Christ.

Although Roberts was unskilled in preaching, the pastor and those seventeen church members began to burn with a fiery touch from God.

The next night more came to hear the young preacher, and the fire quickly spread to other churches. In the next thirty days, thirty-seven thousand came forward to repent of their sins and receive Jesus Christ as their Savior and Lord. Within five months, one hundred thousand were swept into Christ's kingdom across the country, and Roberts' vision was fulfilled.

A newspaper called the *Ram's Horn* reported that Evan Roberts was an unknown, but "then came the summons, and he obeyed. He insists that he has been called to his present work by the direct guidance of the Holy Ghost. At once, without question and without hesitation, he was accepted by the people. Wherever he went, hearts were set aflame with the love of God."[2] The *Methodist Recorder* reported:

> Wales is in the throes and ecstasies of the most remarkable revival it has ever known. It is nothing less than a "moral revolution."[3]

Welsh newspapers began to print lists of names of those being born into the Kingdom of God.

Colleges closed down, and students marched singing and praising God on their way to prayer meetings.

Children held their own meetings in homes and in barnyards, emulating their heroes—the ministers of the churches.

Men's "prayer brigades" began to form. Reports say their prayer was fierce and passionate. One town boasted a "Get-out-of-the-bed" prayer brigade. These men would pray into the night—sometimes all night—for God to rouse other men out of bed, convict them of sin, and save their souls. There were reports of men crawling out of bed in the middle of the night, finding a meeting and crying out to the Lord Jesus to save them.

One account reported that a defendant in court received Christ when the judge and jury stopped to pray over him.

Revival broke out in the coal mines as well. It was reported that the profane language of the miners was so cleaned up that their beasts of burden could no longer understand them—and refused to obey them.

But not everyone was happy with this revival. In a time when clergy viewed religion with an awesome seriousness, some ministers labeled Evan Roberts a youthful seer with unorthodox methods. They could not understand why he smiled when he prayed, or why he laughed when he preached. But those who came to hear him said he had the light of God in his countenance and the joy of the Lord in his heart.

Just as God had shown him, Roberts saw the revival leap to England. There, an estimated two million people received Christ. Then the Holy Spirit coursed out into Western and Northern Europe. When He "fell" upon Norway, so many packed the churches that the clergy had to ordain lay persons in order to serve communion to the masses. Then the Spirit of revival swept across the world to Africa, India, China, and Korea.

In America, ministers tracked the move of God as best they could from sketchy reports from overseas. The excited Americans called clergy meetings in the large cities to decide how to react when the move of God reached their nation. For them, it was not a matter of "if" but "when." And

God rewarded their anticipation: the Spirit came, and His holy fire burned from city to city.

In Atlantic City, New Jersey, in a population of sixty thousand, it was said that "not even fifty" refused to come to the Lord Jesus Christ.

In Paducah, Kentucky, the First Baptist Church added one thousand new converts to its roll; the pastor died, reportedly from exhaustion.

In Burlington, Iowa, every store and factory closed so employees could attend prayer meetings.

In Denver, the mayor declared a day of prayer and by ten in the morning the churches were filled, and another twelve thousand packed downtown theaters and halls.

In Portland, two hundred and forty stores signed an agreement to close from eleven in the morning until two in the afternoon to encourage employees and customers to freely seek God.

In Los Angeles, thousands marched in the streets celebrating the coming of the Holy Spirit, and two hundred thousand gathered for a single open-air meeting.

Historians estimate that twenty million people came to Christ while this revival burned in America.

What Is Revival?

Today, churches declare "revival" if they have a few exciting services. But revival is much more than that. Let us look briefly at some of its characteristics.

First, *revival is a sovereign act of God.* The Holy Spirit used Evan Roberts to trigger a revival in 1904 for which the people of Wales had earnestly prayed since 1901. The praying believers had been cooperating with the Holy Spirit by responding to His work within them. The apostle Paul writes:

> Glory be to God who by his mighty power at work within us is able to do far more than we would ever dare

to ask or even dream of—infinitely beyond our highest prayers, desire, thoughts, or hopes (Ephesians 3:20, TLB).

The Holy Spirit is the one who orchestrates and enables even our love for Christ. We cannot understand God's Word apart from the Holy Spirit who inspired the writing. We cannot pray unless He intercedes for us. We cannot witness for Christ without His power. So revival is the product of the Spirit, the third person of the Trinity.

It was a sovereign act of God when He gave me the vision for Campus Crusade for Christ in 1951. At that moment, I was not even thinking about the Lord. I was studying for a final exam with a friend from Fuller Theological Seminary.

In some ways my experience was similar to the apostle Paul's encounter with the living Christ on the road to Damascus. His companions did not hear the Lord Jesus speak to Paul or see the great light that shown so brightly that Paul was blinded by it. As the Lord spoke to me, a fellow student was sitting at the same table studying but had no idea of what was happening to me. I did not hear a voice, but His message could not have been more real if it had been broadcast over a hundred loud speakers.

After the Holy Spirit gave me the vision, I was so filled with excitement and energy that even my corpuscles were singing praises to God. So I said to my friend, "Let's go for a run!" He ran with me but never understood why I was so filled with joy and praise for God.

Second, *revival is a divine visitation.* In the end, you discover that spiritual renewal was God's idea in the first place. Believers find they were only responding to Him.

Sometimes God comes in power and you have no idea what you said or did to prompt it—and, indeed, it probably had nothing to do with your piety at all.

In 1947, I was in a meeting at Forest Home Christian Conference Center in California. A dear friend of mine, Dr. Henrietta Mears, director of Christian education at the First

Presbyterian Church of Hollywood, was the speaker. Dr. Louis Evans Jr., the son of the senior pastor, and I walked her back to her cabin. We were chatting and enjoying our fellowship, so she invited us in. As we continued to talk, suddenly the Holy Spirit enveloped us. As a young believer, I did not know very much about the person of the Holy Spirit, so I did not know what was happening to me. But I found myself intoxicated with joy. Dr. Evans said it was as though coals of fire ran up and down his spine.

While we were in prayer and praising God, Dr. Richard Halverson entered Dr. Mears' cabin. He was a defeated, frustrated, fruitless, Presbyterian minister from Coalinga, California. He had come to seek her counsel on how he might leave the ministry and return to the Hollywood entertainment world from which he had come before his conversion.

When he walked into the room, we were praying and no one said anything to him. But instantly the Holy Spirit healed him of his defeat and frustration, and his heart was filled with joy and love.

In moments we were all changed. None of us were ever the same again, and God gave each of us major responsibilities in His vineyard. Dr. Evans went on to become a nationally-known Presbyterian minister. For many years he pastored the National Presbyterian Church, "the church of the presidents." Dr. Halverson became chaplain of the U.S. Senate, and for more than thirty years has been recognized as an international Christian statesman. We had all experienced a divine visitation.

Third, *revival is a time of personal humiliation, forgiveness, and restoration* in the Holy Spirit. It is a time when the Spirit calls on a person to repent of obvious sins, and reveals those that are not so obvious—coldness of heart, loss of first love, refusing to step beyond our personal "comfort zones," living quietly as God's "secret agents" in the midst of a society that desperately needs the salt and light of the world. Evangelist James Burns writes:

> [Revival] comes to scorch before it heals; it comes to condemn ministers and people for their unfaithful witness, for their selfish living, for their neglect of the cross, and to call them to daily renunciation, to an evangelical poverty and to a deep and daily consecration. That is why a revival has ever been unpopular with large numbers within the church. Because it says nothing to them of power (worldly ways) such as they have learned to love, or of ease, or of success; it accuses them of sin, it tells them they are dead, it calls them to awake, to renounce the world and to follow Christ.[4]

Fourth, *during revival, preaching is fearless* under the anointing of the Holy Spirit—as in Acts 4:31 when "they spoke the word of God with boldness" (NKJ).

The messages of Jonathan Edwards, a Puritan preacher who eventually became president of Princeton College, is an example. In July 1741, he preached a sermon in Enfield, Connecticut, that ignited The Great Awakening in America. The sermon, "Sinners in the Hands of an Angry God," portrayed hell so clearly that many in his congregation hung onto the pews with whitened knuckles.[5] So great was their conviction of sin at one point that Edwards had to wait quite a while until the people quieted down from their crying out to God for salvation long enough for him to continue. A contemporary of Edwards, Gilbert Tennant, noted that:

> He seemed to have no regard to please the eyes of his hearers with agreeable gesture, nor their ears with delivery, nor their fancy with language; but to aim directly at their heart and consciences, to lay open their ruinous delusions, show them their numerous secret, hypocritical shifts in religion and drive them out of every deceitful refuge wherein they had made themselves easy with the form of godliness without the

power...His preaching was frequently both terrible and searching.[6]

John Wesley, whom God used mightily in revivals in England and America, earlier took a similar approach:

> It was a precept of Wesley to his evangelists in un-folding their message, to speak first in general of the love of God to man; then with all possible energy so as to search the conscience to its depths, to preach the law of holiness; and then, and not till then, to uplift the glories of the gospel of pardon and of life. Intentionally or not, his directions follow the lines of the epistle to the Romans.[7]

Fifth, *the presence of the Holy Spirit is powerful.* Fearless, Christ-centered preaching with people literally "falling on their faces" before God often is a hallmark of revival. In the John Wesley and George Whitefield revivals in England the awesome presence of the Holy Spirit was common and it had a powerful effect on the people. Concerning a White-field revival service, Wesley noted in his journal:

> No sooner had he begun...to invite all sinners to believe in Christ than four persons sunk down close to him, almost in the same moment. One of them lay without sense or motion. A second trembled exceed-ingly. The third had strong convulsions all over his body, but made no noise unless by groans. The fourth, equally convulsed, called upon God with strong cries and tears.[8]

Wesley and Whitefield considered this behavior strange and had some individuals removed from their meetings. But a Lady Huntington wrote to Whitefield, advising him to leave the people alone, because stopping to remove them put a damper on the service. "Let them cry," she said. "It will do a great deal more good than your preaching." And Wesley wrote in his journal:

From this time on, I trust, we shall allow God to carry on His own work in the way that pleases Him.[9]

Concerning the anointing that comes upon revival preachers, Charles Finney said:

If I did not preach from inspiration I didn't know how I did preach. It was a common experience with me...that the subject would open up to my mind in a manner that was surprising to myself. It seemed that I could see with intuitive clearness just what I ought to say, and whole platoons of thoughts, words and illustrations came to me as fast as I could deliver them.[10]

Finney is revered as the father of modern revivalism. When he came to a church, the convicting power of God often caused people to abandon their pews, fall prostrate in the aisle, and moan in repentance.

The late J. Edwin Orr, an eminent authority on revival, reports a different reaction by believers in the revival of 1858:

The most crowded meetings were solemn by their deep and strange stillness. A most thorough conviction and terrible anxiety showed themselves in concentrated meditation and half-suppressed, deep-drawn sighs; while the joy of hope and forgiveness told of its presence by tears, which made the eyes they moistened more radiant than ever.[11]

Some American revivals were marked with miracles and controversial experiences such as trembling, jerking, screaming, groaning, fainting, prostration, or dancing for joy. But the awakening of 1858 saw "quite another series of the gifts of the Spirit [being] multiplied—those of church planter, prophetic exhorter, evangelist, pastor, and teacher. These gifts were in operation among those who received ordination by church authorities, but they were found also in humble laymen whose only ordination was one of the Spirit."[12]

Sixth, *revival changes communities and nations.* American theologian A. W. Tozer defines revival as a move of God that "changes the moral climate of a community."[13] History shows that a true awakening leaps far beyond the walls of any church and radically reforms society.

During the Welsh revival, for example, the social impact was astounding. For a time, crime disappeared: no rapes, no robberies, no murders, no burglaries, no embezzlements— the judges had no cases to try. "The District Consuls held emergency meetings to discuss what to do with the police, now that they were unemployed. Drunkenness was cut in half. The illegitimate birth rate dropped 44 percent in two counties within a year of the beginning of the revival, so great was the impact of the movement."[14]

> *"Study the history of revival. God has always sent revival in the darkest days. Oh for a mighty, sweeping revival today."*
>
> —Dr. Adrian Rogers, pastor
> Bellevue Baptist Church
> Memphis

Revival also shaped the future of America. Fresh from revival in England with John Wesley, the young George Whitefield joined ranks with Jonathan Edwards in New England and took to the open fields with impassioned preaching.

Thousands were converted as he spoke prophetically of "political freedom from the oppression of England as well as the spiritual freedom from the slavery of sin."[15]

While the Holy Spirit burned in men like Edwards and Whitefield, out of a regional population of two hundred and fifty thousand, fifty thousand souls were saved. Added to the number of existing believers, it was enough to "determine the destiny of [our] country."[16]

God used Edwards, Whitefield, and others to turn the colonies back to Him, reestablishing a Christian foundation prior to the Declaration of Independence.

The great Kentucky revival of 1800 swept through Tennessee, North Carolina, South Carolina, and the frontier. Orr reports that out of this awakening "came the whole missionary movement, the abolition of slavery, and popular education. More than six hundred colleges in the Middle West were founded by revivalists."[17]

Our Task

In America today, we need not wait for a sovereign act of God to bring revival. We do not have to wait for a general outpouring of the Holy Spirit on the church and the nation. Our task is to surrender to the Lordship of Christ and the control of the Holy Spirit, fast and pray, and obey God's Word. Meeting these conditions, we can expect the Holy Spirit to transform our lives.

I liken this to the story of two Christian farmers. They lived on adjoining farms. They were both poor when they started, and each had similar equipment. Today one is wealthy, and the other is poor.

The wealthy farmer works hard. He chooses his seed carefully. He fertilizes the soil, waters it, and carefully works the field. And, at the right time, he harvests the grain.

The other farmer is lazy and undisciplined. He does not choose good seed. He does not fertilize his soil properly, and he leaves too much to chance. He loves to sit on his front porch and watch the world pass by on the state highway.

God sends sun and rain on both farms. But he expects the farmers to add shoe leather and elbow grease to what He entrusts to them.

I believe the same is true spiritually. God wants to send revival to the individual who is willing to repent and seek Him. Jesus said:

Blessed are those who hunger and thirst for righteousness, for they will be filled (Matthew 5:6).

God's Word promises us that if we humble ourselves,
reverence and worship God, He will bless us. But for the
slothful person, the disobedient person, there is no blessing—only discipline, or worse.

The Holy Spirit of God is sovereign. He works when and
where He chooses. But we should always pray and plan for
His sovereign work in the affairs of people and nations. But
personal revival begins with an inner call to the heart by the
Holy Spirit (Philippians 2:13; John 16:8–11). The conscience finds itself stirred by that call. The will makes the
decision to obey or ignore it.

Today, our decision is crucial as individuals, as a church,
and as a nation. God is asking us to seek Him with all of our
being. The revival that He promises begins when we humble ourselves, repent, fast, pray, and seek His face and turn
from our evil ways. God has promised to respond with
revival fire for any person who will hear, love, trust, and
obey Him.

CHAPTER 6

Causing the Fire to Fall

By nature, every one of us is inclined to take the path of least resistance. But we Americans are especially notorious for avoiding pain at all cost.

Students shortcut their assigned reading by reviewing study notes. We look for easy exercise programs that won't make us perspire too much.

We are always looking for *the* diet pill that will help us lose weight while enjoying fattening foods. There seems to be a new fad every month for shedding weight without hunger or exercise! Liquid diets and banana diets and protein diets; the list goes on and on.

When it comes right down to it, most of us do not like hard work. Even in those areas that we recognize are in our best interest—like studying, exercise, and diets—we avoid developing disciplines to help us.

This is especially true when it comes to the spiritual discipline of fasting and prayer.

All of us would acknowledge the critical importance of regular fellowship with God. But as I travel around the world and speak to Christians everywhere, I meet very few who express a natural inclination for prayer. And even fewer who include fasting in their discipline.

Yet down through the years, godly people who have done mighty things for God have testified to the necessity of prayer with fasting. John Wesley, who shook the world for God during the Great Awakening that gave rise to the

Methodist Church toward the end of the eighteenth century, is representative of such great spiritual leaders.

John and his brother, Charles Wesley, with their friend George Whitefield and other fellow believers regularly fasted and prayed while students at Oxford University in 1732. These Christian "commoners" studied and worshiped in the midst of mocking young aristocrats who nicknamed them the "Holy Club." Having experienced the spiritual power of fasting and prayer, they carried this discipline into their historic ministries.

John Wesley so believed in this power that he urged early Methodists to fast every Wednesday and Friday. He felt so strongly about fasting those two days a week that he refused to ordain anyone in Methodism unless they agreed to do it.

The roll call of other great Christian leaders who determined to make prayer with fasting a part of their lives reads like a hall of fame: Martin Luther, John Calvin, John Knox, Jonathan Edwards, Matthew Henry, Charles Finney, Andrew Murray, D. Martyn Lloyd-Jones, and many more.

Why were they so convinced of the need for fasting and prayer? And how does fasting cause the fire of God to fall upon the life of the individual and the Church?

Our Need to Fast

The writings of Scripture, the Church Fathers, and many Christian leaders of today offer several biblical insights into the spiritual need for fasting:

- It is a biblical way to truly humble oneself in the sight of God (Psalm 35:13; Ezra 8:21).

- It brings revelation by the Holy Spirit of a person's true spiritual condition, resulting in brokenness, repentance, and change.

- It is a crucial means for personal revival because it brings the inner workings of the Holy Spirit into play in a most unusual, powerful way.

- It helps us better understand the Word of God by making it more meaningful, vital, and practical.

- It transforms prayer into a richer and more personal experience.

- It can result in dynamic personal revival—being controlled and led by the Spirit and regaining a strong sense of spiritual determination.

- It can restore the loss of one's first love for our Lord.

Throughout the Old and New Testament eras and during the last 2,000 years, fasting was a primary means of humbling ourselves before God.

In Isaiah 58:5, the prophet describes fasting as a "day for a man to afflict his soul" (NKJ). In Psalm 69:10, David says he "chastened" his soul with fasting (NKJ). And in Psalm 35:13 he says, "I humbled myself with fasting" (NKJ). Jesus teaches, "Whoever exalts himself will be humbled, and whoever humbles himself will be exalted" (Matthew 23:12). The apostle Peter writes, "Humble yourselves, therefore, under God's mighty hand, that he may lift you up in due time" (1 Peter 5:6). And James admonishes, "Draw nigh to God, and He will draw nigh to you…be afflicted, and mourn, and weep: let your laughter be turned to mourning, and your joy to heaviness. Humble yourselves in the sight of the Lord, and He shall lift you up" (James 4:8–10, KJV).

Fasting reduces the power of self so that the Holy Spirit can do a more intense work within us.

Humility is an attitude of the heart. The Scripture says, "A broken and a contrite heart—these, O God, You will not despise" (Psalm 51:17, NKJ). God will hear us and respond to our cry when we come before Him in humility and brokenness—acknowledging and repenting of our sins, and asking Him to cleanse us by the blood of Jesus and to fill us with His Holy Spirit.

Fasting demonstrates our commitment to Christ. In his book on fasting, Arthur Wallis writes: "When a man is willing to set aside the legitimate appetites of the body to concentrate on the work of praying, he is demonstrating that he means business, that he is seeking with all his heart, and will not let God go unless He answers."[1]

Wallis says Jesus set the example for us. "By His acceptance of those [forty days] of fasting, He was reaffirming His determination to do the will of His Father even to the end."[2]

How Does Fasting Help?

Fasting is a primary means of restoration. By humbling our souls, fasting releases the Holy Spirit to do His special work of revival in us. This changes our relationship with God forever, taking us into a deeper life in Christ and giving us a greater awareness of God's reality and presence in our lives.

Fasting reduces the power of self so that the Holy Spirit can do a more intense work within us. The apostle Paul writes:

> It is God Who is all the while effectually at work in you—energizing and creating in you the power and desire—both to will and to work for His good pleasure and satisfaction and delight (Philippians 2:13, Amplified).

> Now to Him Who, by...the [action of His] power that is at work within us, is able to [carry out His purpose and] do superabundantly, far over and above all that we [dare] ask or think—infinitely beyond our highest prayers, desire, thoughts, hopes or dreams— (Ephesians 3:20, Amplified).

Although these passages do not directly refer to fasting, humbling ourselves before the Lord certainly enlarges the channel of God's power within us. As a result, He can accomplish His will in us and do "superabundantly" more for us than we could ever imagine.

Fasting helps to purify us spiritually. Lee Bueno, author and noted authority on fasting, writes:

> Fasting burns out our selfishness. In fasting we willingly submit to the cauldron of renunciation as we give up one of life's greatest pleasures. Fasting is the foundry in which we are purified. Its fires refine our faith; its flames separate the base impurities from our true character in Christ; its hot blasts purify our hearts.[3]

Fasting increases our spiritual reception by quieting our mind and emotions.

Dr. Julio C. Ruibal, an internationally known nutritionist, pastor, and specialist in fasting and prayer, says our brain is affected by many of our living habits. "Fasting helps to clear up our spiritual reception. It is not that God begins to speak louder when we fast, but we begin to hear Him better."[4]

Fasting also helps in other ways. It:

- Brings a yieldedness, even a holy brokenness, resulting in inner calm and self-control
- Renews spiritual vision
- Inspires determination to follow God's revealed plan for your life

"Fasting," writes Andrew Murray, "helps to express, to deepen, and to confirm the resolution that we are ready to sacrifice everything, [even] ourselves to attain what we seek for the kingdom of God."[5]

When we finish a fast, Lee Bueno says, "We cool into tempered Christians strong with self-control. The dross and cinders of our lustful cravings are skimmed off... [Fasting] produces a work of art—the tempered, selfless Christian—that can be created through no other process of refinement."[6]

Fasting Calls for Sacrifice

The Church of England Homily of 1562 indicates the first purpose of fasting is "to chastise the flesh, that it be not too wanton, but tamed and brought in subjection to the spirit."

Wesleyan preacher William Bramwell wrote in 1809 that the reason many do not live in the power of their salvation is because "there is too much sleep, too much meat and drink, too little fasting and self-denial, too much [taking part in] the world...and too little self-examination and prayer."

We cannot truly humble ourselves before God without personal sacrifice. Lee Bueno writes:

> Humility and self-denial are two sides of the same coin...Jesus' greatest calling [for us] to deny ourselves came when He stated: "If anyone desires to come after Me, let him deny himself, and take up his cross, and follow Me" (Matthew 16:24, NKJ).
>
> By fasting unto the Lord we answer His call to deny ourselves for the sake of the cross.[7]

The apostle Paul, who said he was "in fastings often" (2 Corinthians 11:27, NKJ), also said: "I discipline my body and bring it under subjection" (1 Corinthians 9:27, NKJ). Through such sacrifice, the Holy Spirit provides the fire that purifies the soul.

Fasting Wars Against the Flesh

But for all its spiritual benefits, fasting is not always the easiest godly discipline to practice. For those unaccustomed to it, going without food can be a struggle—a tug of war between the spirit of a person and his flesh.

Bible scholar Adam Clarke, who knew John Wesley and preached for him at meetings, defines "flesh" in his New Testament commentary of 1825 as the old carnal nature, that tendency in every person to gravitate toward the "evil propensities" of the soul.[8]

The flesh does not let go easily. Many have acknowledged a battle in their soul when setting out to fast, especially during the first few days without food.

Paul described this warfare in Galatians 5:17:

> We naturally love to do evil things that are just the opposite from the things that the Holy Spirit tells us to do; and the good things we want to do when the Spirit has his way with us are just the opposite of our natural desires. These two forces within us are constantly fighting each other to win control over us, and our wishes are never free from their pressures (TLB).

He was saying that the flesh *wars* against the Holy Spirit, and the Holy Spirit *wars* against the flesh—"for it is God who works in you to will and to act according to his good purpose" (Philippians 2:13).

The mental and emotional battles that may break out when we fast can sometimes be unsettling. Veteran fasters say this is a sure sign of the need to abstain from food and draw close to God. It means that the natural man, with his appetites and will, is trying to gain ascendancy over the spiritual man and the inner workings of the Holy Spirit.

> *"Eating is the grand-daddy of all appetites. Fasting is a commitment to bring about self-control and overcome every other conceivable temptation."*
>
> —Neil Anderson, president
> Freedom in Christ Ministries

Rees Howells, remembered as the great intercessor of Wales, struggled with fasting when the Holy Spirit first led him to do it at the beginning of his ministry. In his biography, author Norman Grubb quotes him as saying:

My agitation was the proof of the grip it had on me. If the thing had no power over me, why did I argue about it?[9]

Martin Luther, known as "an inveterate faster," said that when he abstained from food for spiritual reasons, his "flesh was wont to grumble dreadfully."[10]

About the control of food over a person, Arthur Wallis writes:

> There are those who are seemingly oblivious to their bondage to food and to the fact that there is here a leakage of spiritual power. They mistake the lust that enslaves them for a natural and healthy appetite. Others are aware but show no alarm that they are slaves of the stomach. The truth that Christian discipleship involves self-discipline in this realm has evidently not penetrated their conscience. Their desire and capacity for food is a big joke. "I can resist anything but temptation," they say.[11]

Fasting Brings Power

The Early Church recognized fasting as a means of obtaining spiritual power. Wallis says:

> Fasting is calculated to bring a note of urgency and [persistence] into our praying, and to give force to our pleas in the court of heaven.[12]

But over the years, Wallis continues, "as spirituality waned and worldliness flourished in the churches, the power and gifts of the Spirit were withdrawn."[13]

This same spiritual erosion can and does occur in the life of the believer today. But God's Word declares fasting and prayer as a powerful means for causing the fire of God to fall again in a person's life.

This fire produces the fruits of the Spirit—love, joy, peace, patience, kindness, goodness, faithfulness, gentleness, and self-control—but especially the fruits of righteousness and spiritual power over the lusts of the flesh and the lies of the enemy.

According to author and teacher Derek Prince, fasting is "a tremendous lesson in establishing who is the master and who is the servant. Remember, your body is a wonderful servant, but a terrible master."[14] And, according to Galatians 5:17, the flesh or carnal nature always strives to be in control.

As fasting and prayer brings surrender of body, soul, and spirit to our Lord and Savior, Jesus Christ, it also generates a heightened sense of the presence of the Holy Spirit; it creates a fresh, clean joy and a restored determination to serve God. In short, it brings personal revival. Our spiritual power does not lie in money, genius, anointed plans, or dedicated work. Rather, power for spiritual conquest comes from the Holy Spirit as people seek God's face in consecrated, diligent prayer and fasting.

In 1954, Roger Bannister broke the four-minute mile. It had never been broken in all the centuries of recorded history, but Bannister believed it could be done. He developed a mental picture of himself breaking the record, and he did it. Since 1954, several hundred other athletes have broken the four-minute mile, simply because Roger Bannister proved that it could be done.

If an individual with only human resources is able to accomplish such remarkable feats, how much more can you and I do when we place our faith in the omnipotent Creator God and draw upon His supernatural, inexhaustible resources and power through fasting and prayer?

The Power of Fasting and Prayer

C an you imagine what would happen if just half the members of your church would earnestly fast and pray with pure hearts and proper motives? You could expect another Pentecost—a miracle of God's grace.

Since Pentecost, the Church has burgeoned from a room full of Jesus' followers to hundreds of millions of Christian believers.

While fasting and prayer are mentioned only twice in the Book of Acts, the discipline apparently was common practice in the Early Church. On one occasion in Antioch while Barnabas, Simeon, Lucius, Manaen, and Saul (later known as Paul) were "worshiping the Lord and fasting," the Holy Spirit spoke to them: "Set apart for me Barnabas and Saul for the work to which I have called them" (Acts 13:1,2). The ordination of these apostles was a significant milestone in the spread of the gospel. Later Luke records that Paul and Barnabas started churches in various cities and, after a time of fasting and prayer, chose elders to oversee the works (Acts 14:21–23).

Today, at this writing, the most powerful movement of God in the world is in Korea. The dynamic, dramatic growth of the Church from three million in 1974 to eleven million in 1990 can be attributed largely to fasting and prayer.

Just picture your church becoming unified in purpose, healed of its wounds, and set on fire for God because a group of dedicated members gathered "in one accord" in humility and earnestness before our Lord to fast and pray.

Richard Foster, a professor at Azusa Pacific University and author of *Celebration of Discipline*, says:

> The group fast can be a wonderful and powerful experience provided there is a prepared people who are of one mind in these matters. Serious problems in churches or other groups can be dealt with and relationships healed through unified group fasting and prayer.[1]

Changing the Destiny of Nations

Not only will fasting and prayer transform an individual or church, it can change the course of a nation.

When Jonah carried God's warning of impending judgment to Nineveh, their king declared a fast. "Let everyone call urgently on God," he commanded. "Let them give up their evil ways and their violence" (Jonah 3:8). Immediately, the people began to mourn over their sins, and their fasting and repentance pleased God's merciful heart.

The writer of the Book of Jonah records, "When God saw what they did and how they turned from their evil ways, he had compassion on them and did not bring upon them the destruction he had threatened" (Jonah 3:10).

We see God's hand of deliverance upon Israel while the nation was in exile in Persia. A wicked man named Haman had risen to great political power and had persuaded the king to destroy all the Jewish people.

> *"The greatest revolution in history would be if 50 percent of Americans who claim to have committed their lives to Christ would turn and begin to follow Jesus."*
>
> —Dr. Paul A. Cedar
> President, Evangelical Free
> Church of America

Unknown to the king, his wife—Queen Esther—was a Jew. She "set an example which became a pattern for all subsequent generations of the power of prayer and fasting" to change history.[2]

Part of the account of how she helped save the Jews is found in Esther 4:15–17:

> Then Esther sent this reply to Mordecai [a Jew pleading with the queen to help her people]: "Go, gather together all the Jews who are in Susa, and fast for me. Do not eat or drink for three days, night or day. I and my maids will fast as you do. When this is done, I will go to the king, even though it is against the law. And if I perish, I perish.

The king's decree made it unlawful for her to approach him unless he sent for her. Esther knew that breaking that law could mean death unless the king nodded his approval when she entered the throne room.

However, after three days of fasting and prayer, Esther went in to see the king. To her relief he smiled his approval. In fact, he was so pleased to see her that he boastfully offered to give her half of his kingdom.

Instead, Esther asked for the lives of the Jews. In the end, the evil Haman was executed and Israel was saved from annihilation.

The power of fasting and prayer is seen again in the time of King Jehoshaphat. The story is told in 2 Chronicles 20:

> Some men came and told Jehoshaphat, "A vast army is coming against you from Edom." Alarmed, Jehoshaphat resolved to inquire of the Lord, and he proclaimed a fast for all Judah. The people of Judah came together to seek help from the Lord; indeed, they came from every town in Judah to seek him (2 Chronicles 20:2–4).

Then the king stood in the assembly of the people at the temple and prayed to God: "We have no power to face this vast army that is attacking us. We do not know what to do, but our eyes are upon you" (2 Chronicles 20:12).

The Holy Spirit responded, speaking through the prophet Jahaziel:

> Do not be afraid or discouraged because of this vast army. For the battle is not yours, but God's...Go out to face them tomorrow, and the Lord will be with you (2 Chronicles 20:15,17).

When the Spirit spoke, "Jehoshaphat bowed with his face to the ground, and all the people of Judah and Jerusalem fell down in worship before the Lord." Then many began to praise God "with a very loud voice" (2 Chronicles 20:18,19).

The next day, the Hebrew army marched out to war, not knowing just what to expect, with their singers in front praising the Lord. And as they marched into battle, the Lord breathed confusion into the camps of the enemy, causing them to attack and destroy each other.

The writer of Chronicles records, "When the men of Judah came to the place that overlooks the desert and looked toward the vast army, they saw only dead bodies lying on the ground; no one had escaped" (2 Chronicles 20:24). Judah's humility in fasting, prayer, and praise had moved the Lord to save His people from sure defeat.

Coursing through the Bible, we find other examples of how fasting often changed the course of events. Moses twice fasted forty days (Deuteronomy 9:9,18) till his face shone with the glory of God. In the time of the judges (Judges 20:26) and in the time of Samuel (1 Samuel 7:6), all Israel fasted. David fasted before he was crowned, when his child was ill, when his enemies were ill (Psalm 35:13), and because of the sins of his people (Psalm 69:9,10). Elijah, Ezra, Nehemiah, Esther, Daniel—all fasted in times of need.

Examples of how fasting and prayer has changed the course of a nation can also be found throughout history. In

1756 the king of England called for a day of solemn prayer and fasting because of a threatened invasion by the French.

About that day, John Wesley wrote in his journal: "The fast day was a glorious day, such as London has scarce seen since the Restoration. Every church in the city was more than full, and a solemn seriousness sat on every face. Surely God heareth prayer, and there will yet be a lengthening of our tranquility."

Later, he added a footnote saying: "Humility was turned into national rejoicing for the threatened invasion by the French was averted."[3]

In 1662, King Charles II of England threatened to take away the Massachusetts Charter if the colony refused to regulate or replace their ministers with Episcopal clergy. When the colony voted unanimously not to comply, the king flew into a rage and vowed to send Colonel Percy "Bloody" Kirk and five thousand troops to crush the opposition.

When Increase Mather, a leading minister, heard the news, he shut himself up in his study and spent the day on his knees fasting and praying about the colony's plight. Finally, Mather's heaviness lifted, replaced by a sense of peace and joy.

Word arrived two months later that Charles II had died of apoplexy. His brother, James II, had become king, and Kirk would not be coming. The death of Charles II was traced back to the day Mather spent in fasting and prayer.[4]

In May 1940, Germany overran Holland and attacked Belgium, driving the opposing French, English, and Belgian forces to the sea. The Germans pursued the French and English across the French frontier with an air, tank, and infantry "blitzkrieg," trapping nearly four hundred thousand Allied forces at Dunkirk.

In desperation, England and France called a national day of prayer for the hopelessly stranded British and French troops. On May 26, the Archbishop of Canterbury led

> *"Satan laughs at our toilings and mocks our tryings, but he shakes when he sees the weakest saint of God on his knees."*
>
> —Dr. Paul A. Cedar
> President, Evangelical Free
> Church of America

prayers from Westminster Abbey. The BBC broadcast the service across the nation. Churches and synagogues everywhere opened their doors for prayer. Shocked at the plight of their soldiers, the British people stopped everything to pray. For the first time in living memory, the famous Petticoat Market was empty on a Sunday so that the market traders could take part in prayer.

As a result, what was almost certain disaster became the Miracle of Dunkirk. For some unexplained reason, Hitler halted the advance of his dreaded panzer division for three days. The normally blustery English Channel remained calm while England evacuated the troops. In spite of heavy air strikes and German bombing, 848 British, French, Dutch, and Belgian vessels rescued about 340,000 Allied soldiers in nine days. Anything that would float—tugboats, yachts, pleasure boats, and naval craft—sailed the English Channel to carry the trapped forces back to England.

On the basis of my knowledge of such urgent prayer events, I can safely assume that the most vital role England and France played in assuring the successful evacuation in spite of impossible conditions was that the people—many of whom fasted and prayed—humbled themselves before God and sought Him for help in time of crisis.

During the Six-Day War of 1967, the chief rabbi of Israel proclaimed a day of fasting concerning the war between the Jews and Arabs.[5] Israel quickly won the war and, in a moment of great prophetic significance, regained control over Jerusalem.

In June 1994, more than a million Christians throughout South Korea gathered in seventy cities to pray for the saturation of their country with the gospel, the fulfillment of the Great Commission, and the reunification of North and South Korea.

I was asked to speak at the Yoida Plaza in Seoul where more than 700,000 gathered for a four-hour praise, fasting, and intercession rally. This was the most earnest prayer meeting in which I have ever participated. Many of the Christians who participated in the citywide prayer meetings fasted for many days preceding and following the event. The meeting at the Yoida Plaza was reminiscent of previous times I have spoken there in 1974 and 1980 when crowds of two to three million gathered each evening for several days.

Shortly after the meetings, the president of North Korea died unexpectedly. Many believe that his death is a major step toward the reunification of their two countries and a direct result of their fasting and prayer.

Warning Before Judgment

The tides of godlessness and lawlessness are rising rapidly in our nation. The sins that led to the Flood of Noah and the destruction of Sodom and Gomorrah have found social acceptance in our society. Clearly, America is ripe for judgment.

But God never sends judgment without fair warning. We see many examples of this in His Word—Adam and Eve, the contemporaries of Noah, Lot regarding the fate of Sodom and Gomorrah, the people of Nineveh, the nation of Israel. But why should God warn those whom He seeks to destroy?

The apostle Peter explains. "The Lord is not slow in keeping his promise, as some understand slowness. He is patient with you, not wanting anyone to perish, but everyone to come to repentance" (2 Peter 3:9).

God's judgments of the past are signs for us today. "God's judgment of Israel is a warning," writes Derek

Prince, "for Western nations where we have a long back-
ground of Christian tradition, knowledge of the Scriptures,
and the organized church. Could it be that God has been
speaking, but we have been deaf as the people of Israel?"[6]

God is merciful. He will withdraw His hand of judgment
if our nation will turn from its wicked way. In his book *God's
Chosen Fast*, Arthur Wallis writes:

> God has inflexible laws dealing with men. Sin is
> visited with judgment, but repentance with mercy. God
> has declared Himself on this point in the plainest of
> terms: "If at any time I declare concerning a nation or
> a kingdom that I will pluck up and break down and
> destroy it, and if that nation, concerning which I have
> spoken, turns from its evil, I will repent of the evil that
> I intended to do to it" (Jeremiah 18:7,8, RSV).[7]
>
> [But even if] heaven has issued the decree and the
> wheels are already in motion, there is still a mighty
> weapon to which we may have recourse.[8]

That mighty weapon is repentance, fasting, and prayer.
God promises to hear from heaven, forgive our sins, and
heal our land (2 Chronicles 7:14) if we as a nation are
obedient to that call.

It will take nothing short of the supernatural to stem the
tides of judgment devastating our land. I believe that nothing else can compare with the supernatural power released
when we fast and pray. We know for certain from Hebrews
11:6 and from personal experience that God rewards those
who diligently seek Him.

CHAPTER 8

"You Want Me to Fast?"

To most Christians, fasting means giving up candy bars or sodas for Lent. Or perhaps going without fatty foods and sugar as part of a diet. The very thought of not eating at all can send chills up their spine.

Because prayer with fasting is not a usual practice in churches today, believers quickly shy away from it.

"*Me* fast?"

"Go without food?"

"Starve myself?"

"What possibly for?"

And those who even consider fasting unto the Lord want satisfactory answers to questions like these:

"Won't I get sick?"

"Should I consult my doctor first?"

"Will God always give me what I want if I add fasting to my prayers?"

Let me share with you some of the most common objections and questions that people have about a spiritual fast.

"If I'm supposed to fast, why do I never hear about it at church?"

The Early Church followed in the footsteps of our Lord and the apostles with prayer and fasting. But by medieval times, fasting as a discipline came to be frowned upon. Believers saw it as a severe, ascetic practice better suited for monks in monasteries. For a century, fasting has lain rusting and forgotten in a dark corner of the Church.

Fasting as a discipline—except for those who know its special benefits—is still frowned upon. Bible commentator Matthew Henry wrote, "Fasting is a laudable practice, and we have reason to lament...that it is so neglected among Christians."[1]

In our time, the idea of fasting and prayer does not enter the mind of most Christians. Bible teacher Derek Prince says: "Fasting is a lost key, [a grace] that is found through all the pages of the Bible. Yet it has been set aside and misplaced by the Christian church."[2] Professor Richard Foster sums up the problem today:

> In a culture where the landscape is dotted with shrines to the Golden Arches and an assortment of Pizza Temples, fasting seems out of place, out of step with the times. In fact, fasting has been in general disrepute both in and outside the Church for many years. For example, in my research I could not find a single book published on the subject of Christian fasting from 1861 to 1954, a period of nearly one hundred years. More recently a renewed interest in fasting has developed, but we have far to go to recover a biblical balance.[3]

"Does the Bible really say that we should fast?"

Fasting is mentioned frequently in God's holy Word.[4] Often it is associated with weeping and other acts of humility before God. In Joel 2:12,13 the Lord commanded:

> Return to me with all your heart, with fasting and weeping and mourning. Rend your heart and not your garments. Return to the Lord your God...

God called on His people to fast for cleansing of sin on the Day of Atonement, which practicing Jews celebrate as Yom Kippur:

> And this shall be a permanent statute for you: in the seventh month, on the tenth day of the month, you shall humble your souls, and not do any work, whether the native, or the alien who sojourns among you; for it is on this day that atonement shall be made for you to cleanse you; you shall be clean from all your sins before the Lord (Leviticus 16:29,30, NASB).

Derek Prince comments, "We know, historically, that for 3,000 years the Jewish people have always observed Yom Kippur...as a day of fasting. We also have the New Testament authority for this. A passage in Acts that describes Paul's journey to Rome by sea says:

> Much time had been lost, and sailing had already become dangerous because by now it was after the Fast (Acts 27:9).

"The 'Fast' mentioned here is the Day of Atonement, which always fell at the end of September or the beginning of October, just when winter [sic] was setting in...God required His people to humble their souls before Him in collective fasting. That was the appointment, the ordinance, for the Day of Atonement, the most sacred day of the Jewish calendar.

"Notice two facts: First, in this case, fasting was man's response to God's provision of forgiveness and cleansing. God provided the ceremony by which the High Priest went into the innermost sanctuary of the temple and made atonement. Second, that atonement *was only effective for those people who accepted it through fasting.*"[5]

A similar situation exists in the New Testament concerning repentance of sins. In James 4:8–10, the Scripture says:

> Wash your hands, you sinners, and purify your hearts, you double-minded. Grieve, mourn and wail. Change your laughter to mourning and your joy to gloom. Humble yourselves before the Lord, and he will lift you up.

In the Old Testament, fasting was the way the people individually and collectively humbled themselves (see Psalm 35:13, Psalm 69:10, Isaiah 58:5, and Joel 2:12–17). God's people have always fasted to humble themselves, to receive cleansing of their sins by effective repentance, for spiritual renewal, and for special helps. As we saw earlier, Ezra called a fast to seek God's protection for the Jews returning from Babylon to Jerusalem (Ezra 8:21).

Concerning Ezra, Edith Schaeffer writes in *The Life of Prayer:*

> This serious fasting and prayer, bowing humbly before God with repentance and concern for His mercy, took place in the context of practical need—for protection and guidance, for help in choices and for the supply of material things.[6]

In the New Testament, Luke records the account of a prophetess named Anna who in her eighties "never left the temple but worshiped night and day, fasting and praying" (Luke 2:36,37).

Jesus set the example by fasting forty days after His baptism. For Jesus it was a matter of *when* believers would fast, not *if* they would do it. He spoke in these terms:

> When you give to the needy,…When you pray,… When you fast,… (Matthew 6:2,5,16).

He also said:

> How can the guests of the bridegroom mourn while he is with them? The time will come when the bridegroom will be taken from them; then they will fast (Matthew 9:15).

Jesus is the bridegroom. The guests of the bridegroom represent His followers, all Christians. "Will be taken" refers to our Lord's death, resurrection, and ascension into heaven. Fasting, Jesus was saying, is one of the disciplines of Christian life as we carry on the work of His kingdom.

"It was not Christ's intention to reject or despise fasting," Martin Luther wrote. "It was His intention to restore *proper* fasting."[7]

Prophets and teachers fasted at Antioch (Acts 13:2) and Paul—who wrote much of the New Testament—said he was "in fastings often" (2 Corinthians 11:27, NKJ).

For believers, then, the question is not *Should I fast?*, but *Will I fast?*

"But is fasting a commandment? Where does God make it clear that He requires us to fast today?"

This is a controversial issue. Theologians who believe in fasting differ. "Fasting," argued Thomas Cartwright, "is an abstinence *commanded* of the Lord, to make solemn profession of our repentance." John Brown, on the other hand, did not believe Christ commanded the practice "but proceeded on the principle that the children of the kingdom would perform [it]."[8]

After examining the laws of the Old Covenant and the teachings of the New Covenant, David R. Smith concludes:

> The Jews were commanded to fast in Old Testament times, in a prescribed manner, (but) there is no similar command to Christians.[9]

But he adds:

> Early law was but a type of that which was to be written on the hearts of believers, after they had experienced the New Birth...although fasting is not commanded in the New Testament, it is a duty which Christians do perform.[10]

Other authoritative sources agree with this position. Not one argues against spiritual fasting for today. Rather, all encourage it as a grace God has provided for the revival of the individual and the Church.

"Isn't fasting practiced by ungodly religions?"

Fasting is not exclusive to Christianity. The discipline is found in all the major religions of the world. Zoroaster, Confucius, the Yogis of India, Plato, Socrates, Aristotle—even Hippocrates, the father of modern medicine—believed in fasting.

But Christians are the only ones who fast unto the Creator God, the Father of our Lord and Savior Jesus Christ. Christians, therefore, are the only ones who can know the blessings of God that come from spiritual fasting. Others practice it for vain religious reasons or to improve their health.

"I just don't feel the need to fast!"

This may be an honest admission, but many believers who say this are at the same time calling out for spiritual guidance and power in their lives. By neglecting fasting and prayer, they are blocking a dynamic means by which the Holy Spirit brings the changes they so earnestly desire.

How you feel has little to do with your *need* to fast and pray. Once you learn to fast, you will notice the dramatic *before* and *after* spiritual difference. And as you grow in faith, you will begin to feel the need to fast.

"I just don't have the time!"

Time is a gift from God. Every second of every minute, every minute of every hour, twenty-four hours a day, belong to Him. Each of us has enough time to do what we believe is important.

Let me encourage you to evaluate everything you do. You may be surprised at how much time you really have. Examine your calendar. How much time do you waste on selfish pursuits? Do you squander many hours watching television programs or reading books that have no edifying merit or spiritual benefit? Are you using your time in selfish leisure or personal pleasure beyond your reasonable needs?

How much of this time can you dedicate to fasting and prayer?

I encourage you to prayerfully consider giving a tithe of your day, week, or month to the Lord in fasting and prayer. You will be amazed at how much more you will accomplish in the remaining nine-tenths. Results will show in various ways. God will help you increase your efficiency. Others may offer to help you with a time-consuming project. The demands on your time may lessen. Certainly you will discover that your other Christian duties will increase in fruitfulness, and you will be more effective in sharing your faith with your loved ones, friends, and neighbors.

"How does fasting 'unto the Lord' benefit me spiritually?"

Charles Spurgeon noted, "Our seasons of fasting and prayer at the Tabernacle have been high days indeed; never has Heaven's gate stood wider; never have our hearts been nearer the central Glory."[11]

The apostle James says, "Come near to God and he will come near to you. Humble yourselves before the Lord, and he will lift you up" (James 4:8,10). A humble heart is repentant, dependent upon the Holy Spirit, grateful, forgiving, obedient, respectful, and willing to serve. It has been my experience—and that of others who have earnestly sought God—that prayer with fasting intensifies these and other inner workings of the Holy Spirit.

Fasting prepares us for the deepest and richest spiritual communion possible. It clears and liberates our minds to understand what God is saying to our spirits. It conditions our bodies to carry out His perfect will.

When we persevere through the initial mental and physical discomforts, we will experience a calming of the soul and cooling of the appetites. As a result we will sense the presence of the Lord more than ever before. We will see the fruit of His Holy Spirit evidenced in a fresh, new way (Galatians 5:22,23).

Fasting with a pure heart and motives, I have discovered, brings personal revival and adds power to our prayers. Personal revival occurs because fasting is an act of humility. Fasting gives opportunity for deeper humility as we recognize our sins, repent, receive God's forgiveness, and experience His cleansing of our soul and spirit. Fasting also demonstrates our love for God and our full confidence in His faithfulness.

Since spiritual fasting helps bring the soul in tune with God, it enables us to meet His conditions for answered prayer. The Scripture says:

> Beloved, if our heart does not condemn us, we have confidence toward God. And whatever we ask we receive from Him, because we keep His commandments and do those things that are pleasing in His sight (1 John 3:21,22, NKJ).

Many who write about the values of fasting point to increased effectiveness in intercessory prayer, deliverance from bondage, and guidance in decisions.

In my own experience, fasting greatly enhances my daily fellowship with God in a relationship that has always been very meaningful to me since our Savior changed my life in 1944. Although I have always loved to read God's Word, my forty-day fast resulted in an even more exciting discovery of many golden nuggets of truth that I had not seen before. My prayer life continues to be more exciting. I find I can hardly wait to see how God is going to answer specific prayers.

"Will God always answer and give me what I ask if I add fasting to my prayers?"

No. He will not always give you what you want just because you fast. We cannot barter with God. He only answers prayers that are in harmony with His will and purpose for our lives. The Scripture gives us this promise:

> This is the confidence that we have in Him, that if we ask anything according to His will, He hears us.
>
> And if we know that He hears us, whatever we ask, we know that we have the petitions that we have asked of Him (1 John 5:14,15, NKJ).

About getting what you want by fasting, Edith Schaeffer writes:

> Is fasting ever a bribe to get God to pay more attention to the petitions? No, a thousand times no. It is simply a way to make clear that we sufficiently reverence the amazing opportunity to ask help from the everlasting God, the Creator of the universe, to choose to put everything else aside and concentrate on worshiping, asking for forgiveness, and making our requests known—considering His help more important than anything we could do ourselves in our own strength and with our own ideas.[12]

Adding to these thoughts, Wesley L. Duewel writes in *Touch the World Through Prayer:*

> Fasting in the biblical sense is choosing not to partake of food because your spiritual hunger is so deep, your determination in intercession so intense, or your spiritual warfare so demanding that you have temporarily set aside even fleshly needs to give yourself to prayer and meditation.[13]

God sovereignly watches over us for our ultimate good (Romans 8:28); He works in us to do *His* will (Philippians 2:13). And you can always expect God to respond to you when you submit to Him (James 4:6,8,10). He will always do something special for you—inwardly or outwardly or both—when you deny yourself and focus your love, worship, adoration, faith, and obedience solely toward Him.

"Do I fast for blessings for myself or for someone else?"

Praying for ourselves and interceding for others are among the reasons we should fast and pray. I encourage you to bring your personal needs before the Lord, to intercede for your loved ones, your friends, your church, your community, our nation, and the world—and that the Great Commission will be fulfilled.

True spiritual fasting, however, focuses on God. Our prayers bring results only when our hearts are pure and our motives are unselfish. This can only take place if God and His holy Word are at the center of our attention.

Our motive for fasting is vital. "If our fasting is not unto God," Richard Foster says, "we have failed. Physical benefits, success in prayer, the enduing with power, spiritual insights—these must never replace God as the center of our fasting."[14]

"Like that apostolic band at Antioch," Foster says, "'fasting' and 'worshiping the Lord' must be said in the same breath (Acts 13:2)."[15] John Wesley declared:

> First, let [fasting] be done unto the Lord with our eye singly fixed on Him. Let our intention herein be this, and this alone, to glorify our Father which is in heaven.[16]

"I'm thinking about fasting, but how do I know when I am supposed to do it?"

Some teach that you should *always* be led or prompted by the Holy Spirit to fast. But being "led" by the Spirit and "hearing" the Spirit is a highly subjective, personal area of the Christian life. Believers do not always "hear" accurately, especially if it is something they do not want to do.

The flesh will surely try to override inner promptings to abstain from food. God may be calling you to fast, but the flesh may be saying, "That's just your imagination. How is fasting going to help you in this situation?"

Once you learn the purpose and benefits of fasting, you are free to "proclaim" a fast whenever you sense the desire to draw close to God in a dynamic way or feel the need to seek special help from Him.

Those who consistently practice fasting know instinctively when to do so. They recognize certain spiritual conditions and life circumstances as the signal to get serious with God and increase their spiritual focus. I try to live according to Philippians 2:13, "It is God who works in you to will and to act according to his good purpose."

The still, small voice of the Spirit, always consistent with the Word of God, will tell you what to do if you will only learn to listen.

Author R. D. Chatham tells of a pastor's wife who kept a diary of her fasts. She recorded how she and her husband were changing pastorates and felt overwhelmed by their new responsibilities and realized they needed God's help. Together they fasted ten days. She said that if she had not fasted—and received special strength from the Lord—she would have "gone under."[17]

There are times, however, when the Holy Spirit will prompt you to fast. On another page in her diary, the pastor's wife reported, "Monday: I awoke feeling the need to go on a fast."[18] This prompting can come any time, any place.

It is particularly important to receive a leading of the Lord before beginning an extended spiritual fast. If you undertake a long fast simply on your own, you may run into difficulties. But if the Lord leads you into a protracted fast, He will give you the strength to carry it out.

God impressed me for several months that He wanted me to fast forty days. But as I have said before, I was not sure I could fast that long. Even so, I began my fast with the prayer, "Lord, I will fast as long as You will enable me. I am looking to You to help me. I am claiming Your promise recorded in Isaiah 40:31, 'Those who wait on the Lord shall renew their strength; they shall mount up with wings like eagles, they shall run and not be weary, they shall walk and not faint'" (NKJ). God was faithful to His promise. My fast was the greatest forty days of my life spiritually.

"Is it possible for a Christian to get 'caught up' in fasting and go too far with it?"

We should think of spiritual fasting in terms of *balance*. More fasting does not automatically mean more spiritual benefits. Once you persevere in prayer to a place of victory, and God's purposes for you have been accomplished for the moment, you do not need to immediately plan for another fast.

Spiritual fasting is not a lifestyle in itself, although it should definitely be a part of your Christian walk.

"Do I need an organized plan for my fasting or a schedule to follow?"

David R. Smith writes, "A mature Christian, who has no difficulty about missing meals, does not need to have an organized plan and may not need to have even a day of fasting every week; his fasting will be a personal matter between himself and his Lord and it will follow the pattern which his prayer life suggests to him is proper."[19] But this presupposes a genuine willingness to hear and obey the Lord.

For the purpose of spiritual discipline, John Wesley fasted each Wednesday and Friday.[20] This was in addition to longer fasts for special purposes.

In the final analysis, Christians are not under the Law of the Old Testament and the New Testament does not command fasting on certain days. As with what we eat (Romans 14), fasting is left up to us as a matter of faith.

Once you understand the purpose of fasting and realize what it does for you, however, regular fasting will begin to make spiritual sense. The more you fast for the purpose of seeking God's face and for His glory, the more you will want to fast. The rewards and benefits are rich beyond measure.

"Should I consult my doctor before I fast?"

I recommend it. Unfortunately, many doctors have not been trained in this area and so their understanding is limited.

In writing this book, the subject of doctors has been a chief concern. Author Lee Bueno, who conducts seminars on the physical and spiritual benefits of fasting, makes a strong statement about the attitude of doctors toward fasting:

> All but one in a thousand doctors react negatively to the subject of fasting. They have never fasted, know little about the subject, and respond only to bizarre stories that they've heard. Lack of understanding creates unnecessary fear and results in unfounded, imaginary dangers and the use of scare tactics by doctors to [make you] avoid fasting.[21]

In spite of this, I encourage you to consult with your physician before beginning an extended fast. And I strongly suggest that you ask for a physical exam to make sure you are in good health. You may have a physical problem that could make fasting dangerous and unwise. But be forewarned: your doctor may try to discourage you from fasting, even if you are in good health. If this happens, you may be faced with a dilemma similar to mine.

Over the years, I have fasted many times—often from one to four weeks at a time—without consulting a physician. Since my forty-day fast was beyond anything I had ever undertaken, I called several Christian and secular doctors for their advice. They either knew nothing about fasting or tried to discourage me altogether, and I realized that I was on my own. Would I obey the Holy Spirit or what those doctors had to say?

Authorities on fasting agree that if you know that you are healthy and you fast properly, you will benefit physically as well as spiritually.[22]

Although I ate no solid foods for forty days, I supplemented my distilled-water intake with various kinds of fruit juices. As a result, I actually felt better physically than I did before I began my fast. However, an extended fast on water alone should be conducted with great caution and much prayer. Without proper counsel and supervision, such a fast can be very dangerous.

There are certain persons who should never fast without professional supervision:

- Persons who are physically emaciated

- Those who suffer weakness or anemia

- Persons who have tumors, bleeding ulcers, cancer, blood diseases, or who have recently suffered myocardial infarction

- Those who suffer chronic problems with kidneys, liver, lungs, heart, or other important organs

- Individuals who take insulin for diabetes, or suffer any other blood sugar problem such as hypoglycemia

- Women who are pregnant or nursing[23]

- Those who are afraid of fasting because they do not understand its benefits or what to expect, and who may even believe it amounts to starvation. Fasting is not starvation,[24] but if a person has genuine doubts and emotions—which must be overcome—no persuasion should cause them to fast until they learn what they need to know.

There may be persons with other conditions who should not fast. The rule of thumb is this: If you have serious questions about your health, or if you are under a physician's care, you should consult your doctor before you abstain from food or change your diet.

"How does God want me to fast?"

"In Scripture the *normal* means of fasting involves abstaining from all food, solid or liquid, but not from water," says Richard Foster. "From a physical standpoint, this is usually what is involved in a fast."[25]

The Bible mentions three kinds of fasts: *partial, absolute,* and *supernatural absolute.*

The *partial* fast is described in the book of Daniel. Although the water fast seemed to be the custom of the prophet, there was a three-week period in which he only abstained from "delicacies," meat, and wine (Daniel 10:3).

Lee Bueno says, "The juice diet is the most popular form of the partial fast. [This] means abstinence from certain select foods and drinks, but not complete abstinence from all foods and drinks..."[26]

I began my forty-day fast on a liquid formula that I have found effective over the years: one gallon of distilled water with 1½ cups of lemon juice and a ½ cup of maple syrup added to it, plus ¼ teaspoon of cayenne pepper. The lemon juice adds flavor and Vitamin C, the maple syrup provides energy, and the cayenne pepper—an herb—acts to open small blood vessels which, I believe, helps the body as it cleanses itself of stored toxins.

(*A word of caution:* Although I used this formula with no ill effects, cayenne pepper could cause severe physical reactions in persons allergic to this herb.[27])

For twenty days of my fast, I drank distilled water and a variety of fruit and vegetable juices. For those unaccustomed to fasting, I recommend vegetable and fruit juices along with water.[28] The juices provide strength, and they give you something to look forward to, which helps to alleviate the mental stress that comes from knowing that you are not going to eat that day. I find it helpful to keep the water or juices beside me for frequent sipping throughout the day.

The *absolute* and the *supernatural absolute*[29] are total fasts, meaning no food—solid or liquid—and no water.

Paul went on an absolute fast for three days following his encounter with Jesus on the road to Damascus (Acts 9:9). Esther called for an absolute fast for three days when the Jews faced annihilation in the Persian Empire (Esther 4:16).

> "When I fast unto the Lord ...I can expect a supernatural supply of energy."
>
> —*Bill Bright*

Moses and Elijah engaged in what must be considered a supernatural absolute fast of forty days (Deuteronomy 9:9; 1 Kings 19:8).[30]

But because of dehydration, I do not recommend these types of fasts. They can be dangerous to your health. I strongly advise you to drink plenty of liquids. Obviously, if God leads you to undertake an absolute or supernatural absolute fast, you must obey. However, I strongly encourage you to be certain without doubt that God is leading you.

"What about work and normal duties? Should I take time off to fast?"

How long you fast, the kind of fast you undertake, and whether you adjust your work schedule depends mostly on your occupation. Persons with office jobs, pastors, or housewives—unlike those who perform heavy manual labor—may naturally find it easier to continue their duties and fast longer periods of time.

I agree with Arthur Wallis who writes, "There should be no difficulty in undertaking a day's fast, whatever one's occupation." He has known "housewives and mothers who have profited from a fast of three days or longer while running the home... [and] manual workers who have undertaken longer fasts with no ill effects, but one would not normally recommend it."[31]

Remember, you are fasting unto the Lord. You need special time alone with Him in prayer and in meditation on God's Word. Lee Bueno says:

> Some people combine [fasting] with a heavy work load. Most of them wonder why their time didn't yield results. "What happened?" they innocently ask, never realizing that their attention had been divided between God and the world the whole time.[32]

When I fasted forty days, I shortened my work schedule at Campus Crusade to make more time available to read God's Word, pray, and seek God's face. Actually, even my speaking engagements and other projects seemed to take on the aspect of worship and became an offering unto the Lord.

A spiritual fast supersedes anything done in the "natural." When I fast unto the Lord, spending time in prayer and God's Holy Word, I can expect a supernatural supply of energy. The inner working of the Holy Spirit underscores the Scripture that says, "God is able to make all grace abound to you" (2 Corinthians 9:8).

But not everyone "glides" through a fast without problems. One of my colleagues who fasted one meal each day during my forty-day period experienced spiritual conflict. Another colleague unwisely undertook a total fast with water only, while continuing his usual schedule of work.

"I thought I was going to die," he said. "I really felt that I was at the point of physical breakdown."

"Will fasting ruin my health?"

This is a legitimate concern because of the limited teaching on the subject. But most nutritionists and health specialists who are knowledgeable about fasting can document hundreds, even thousands, of examples where fasting has been physically rejuvenating.[33]

Christian nutritionist Dr. Julio C. Ruibal, says:

Fasting is a natural physiological process. It is also a biblical concept that was practiced during difficult times. So, from both the scriptural and the scientific point of view, we can have confidence that fasting is not harmful, but rather beneficial when properly carried out.[34]

From my experience, arthritic pains in my thumb and fingers were greatly lessened after fourteen to twenty-one days of fasting. Because of a hiatal hernia, I have taken several antacid tablets each day for years to help ease stomach discomfort. But, I did not require one tablet during my entire fast. Now that I am back on a normal diet, however, I find it necessary to take the antacid tablets again.

By fasting we present our bodies "as living sacrifices, holy and pleasing to God" (Romans 12:1). We crucify our sinful desires so that we can more effectively serve God and fulfill His will in our lives.

Nothing can compare with fasting and prayer to bring personal revival and renewal to the Church. I believe the next move of God, which is now under way, will restore biblical fasting to the body of Christ.

CHAPTER 9

Preparing for Your Fast

H onest, I really don't know how to seek God in fasting and prayer. I go to church, read my Bible and pray a little, but that's about it."

"I want to fast and pray, but I've never fasted before. Will I still be able to work every day?"

"Listen, if I have my mind on food all the time, how am I going to do my work? How am I really going to honor and worship God?"

"I'm really afraid of fasting. Will it make me grumpy? How will I cope with the kids?"

Perhaps like most Christians you have similar concerns about fasting. You wonder, "How do I begin? Should I go without food entirely? If so, do I drink only water, or are other liquids okay? How long should I fast and how can I maintain a fast? May I keep walking and jogging? Do I need extra rest? May I tell others what I am doing? How do I fast, pray, seek God, and go about my daily duties—all at the same time? What should I do when it's time to end my fast? What kind of change can I expect in my life?"

In this chapter, we will look at practical answers to these questions, and I will share several guidelines to help you conduct your fast in a safe and spiritually rewarding manner.

Your Call to Fast

Your first move toward fasting and prayer begins with an awareness of your need to do it. Consider the information contained in this book as the "call" of the Holy Spirit for you to fast and pray.

The more you learn about fasting and its special spiritual and physical benefits, the easier it will be for the Holy Spirit to prompt you to fast and pray. Working within us, the Holy Spirit seldom speaks in a loud, dramatic way. Instead, according to Philippians 2:13, He may simply make you *aware* of your need to fast. You may sense an inner urge to seek God in a special way. The Holy Spirit may also use a compelling circumstance or a desperate need as a means of calling you to fast and pray.

For several months before I undertook my forty-day fast, the Holy Spirit had burdened my heart with the rapidly disintegrating moral and spiritual condition of this nation. My heart had grieved over America for at least thirty years, but this was a fresh and special working of the Holy Spirit. He was leading me to "seek God's face" in a depth of prayer far beyond anything I had ever done.

How to Begin

How you begin and conduct your fast will largely determine your success. Permit me to suggest steps to take that will help make your time with the Lord more meaningful and spiritually rewarding, while at the same time enhancing your physical health.

First, *set a specific objective*. Why are you fasting? Is it for spiritual renewal, for guidance, for healing, for the resolution of problems, for special grace to handle a difficult situation? Keeping your goal in focus will help you sustain your fast when physical temptations and life's pressures tempt you to abandon it.

I personally believe the Holy Spirit has given all believers an urgent call to humble ourselves through fasting and prayer so that He may stir our souls, awaken our churches, and heal our land according to 2 Chronicles 7:14. *I urge you to make this your primary purpose for fasting.*

Laying Your Spiritual Foundation

Second, *prepare yourself spiritually*. The very foundation of fasting and prayer is repentance. Unconfessed sin will hinder your prayers. In Scripture, God always requires His people to repent of their sins before He will hear their prayers. David said:

> Come and hear, all of you who reverence the Lord, and I will tell you what he did for me: For I cried to him for help, with praises ready on my tongue. He would not have listened if I had not confessed my sins. But he listened! He heard my prayer! He paid attention to it!
>
> Blessed be God who didn't turn away when I was praying, and didn't refuse me his kindness and love (Psalm 66:16–20, TLB).

In another passage, David shares the joy that returned to him after he confessed his sins, including adultery and murder.

> What happiness for those whose guilt has been forgiven! What joys when sins are covered over! What relief for those who have confessed their sins and God has cleared their record. There was a time when I wouldn't admit what a sinner I was. But my dishonesty made me miserable and filled my days with frustration. All day and all night your hand was heavy upon me. My strength evaporated like water on a sunny day until I finally admitted all my sins to you and stopped trying to hide them. I said to myself, "I will confess them to the Lord." And you forgave me! All my guilt is gone. Now I say that each believer should confess his sins to God when he is aware of them, while there is time to be forgiven. Judgment will not touch him if he does (Psalm 32:1–6, TLB).

And Solomon records:

> The Lord is far from the wicked but he hears the prayer of the righteous (Proverbs 15:29).

As you begin your fast, I encourage you to confess every known sin that the Holy Spirit calls to your remembrance. Include obvious sins, and those that are not so apparent, such as leaving your first love for our Lord, worldly-mindedness, self-centeredness, and spiritual indifference—being unwilling to share your faith in Christ with others, unwilling to help at church, unwilling to spend time in God's Word and in prayer.

Include sins against our country—such as failing to vote, complacency on moral and spiritual values, or cheating on your income tax. Ask the Holy Spirit to reveal anything in your heart that is not pleasing to God.

> *The very foundation of fasting and prayer is repentance. Unconfessed sin will hinder your prayers.*

Perhaps He will remind you of something you said that has hurt someone or damaged their reputation; or your lack of trust in God that is keeping you from fully surrendering your will to Him. List the sins on a sheet of paper and claim His promise recorded in 1 John 1:9, "If we confess our sins, he is faithful and just and will forgive us our sins and purify us from all unrighteousness."

One of the most important truths of Scripture—the understanding and application of which has enriched my life as has no other truth—is a concept that I call "Spiritual Breathing."

Like physical breathing, Spiritual Breathing is a process of exhaling the impure and inhaling the pure. If you sin by committing a deliberate act of disobedience, breathe spiritually to restore the fullness of God's Holy Spirit in your life.

You exhale by confession. As God's Word promises, if we confess our sins, He will forgive us. In the Greek, the original language of the New Testament, the word "confess" *(homologeo)* means to "agree with" or to "say along with." Such agreement involves several considerations.

You first acknowledge that your sin or sins—which should be named to God specifically—are wrong and are therefore grievous to Him.

Evelyn Christenson, internationally known authority on prayer, provides a list[1] of possible sins that may help you. Every "yes" answer is a sin in your life that needs to be confessed.

- *In everything give thanks; for this is the will of God in Christ Jesus for you (1 Thessalonians 5:18, NKJ).*

  Do you worry about anything? Have you failed to thank God for *all* things, the seemingly bad as well as the good? Do you neglect to give thanks at mealtime?

- *Now to him who is able to do exceedingly abundantly above all that we ask or think, according to the power that works in us (Ephesians 3:20, NKJ).*

  Do you fail to attempt things for God because you are not talented enough? Do feelings of inferiority keep you from trying to serve God? When you do accomplish something for Christ, do you fail to give Him all the glory?

- *You shall receive power when the Holy Spirit has come upon you; and you shall be witnesses to Me in Jerusalem, and in all Judea and Samaria, and to the end of the earth (Acts 1:8, NKJ).*

  Have you failed to be a witness with your life for Christ? Have you felt it was enough to just live your Christianity and not witness with your mouth to the lost?

- *I say . . . to everyone who is among you, not to think of himself more highly than he ought to think (Romans 12:3, NKJ).*

  Are you proud of *your* accomplishments, *your* talents, *your* family? Do you fail to see others as better than yourself, more important than yourself in the body of

Christ? Do you think that as a Christian you are doing quite well? Do you rebel at God wanting to change you?

- *Let all bitterness, wrath, anger, clamor, and evil speaking be put away from you, with all malice (Ephesians 4:31, NKJ).*

  Do you complain, find fault, argue? Do you have a critical spirit? Do you carry a grudge against Christians of another group because they don't see eye to eye with you on all things? Do you speak unkindly about people when they are not present? Are you angry with yourself? Others? God?

- *Do you not know that your body is the temple of the Holy Spirit who is in you, whom you have from God, and you are not your own (1 Corinthians 6:19, NKJ)?*

  Are you careless with your body? Are you guilty of not caring for it as the temple of the Holy Spirit in eating and exercise habits? Do you defile your body with unholy sex acts?

- *Let no corrupt communication proceed out of your mouth (Ephesians 4:29, NKJ).*

  Do you ever use filthy language, tell slightly off-color jokes? Do you condone others doing so in your presence, in your home?

- *Do not . . . give place to the devil (Ephesians 4:26,27, NKJ).*

  Do you fail to see that you are a "landing strip" for Satan when you open your mind to him through Transcendental Meditation, yoga, psychic predictions, occult literature, and violent, sex-driven movies? Do you get advice for daily living from horoscopes rather than from God? Do you let Satan use you to thwart the cause of Christ in your church through criticism, gossip, and non-support?

- *Not slothful in business (Romans 12:11, KJV).*

  Do you fail to pay your debts on time? Avoid paying them altogether? Do you charge more on credit cards than you can pay when due? Do you neglect to keep honest income tax records? Do you engage in any shady business deals?

- *Not forsaking the assembling of ourselves together (Hebrews 10:25, NKJ).*

  Are you irregular or spasmodic in church attendance? Do you attend preaching services in body only, whispering, reading, or planning while God's Word is being preached? Are you skipping prayer meetings? Have you neglected family devotions?

- *Do not lie to one another, since you have put off the old man with his deeds (Colossians 3:9, NKJ).*

  Do you ever lie? Exaggerate? Do you fail to see "little white lies" as sin? Do you tell things the way you want them rather than the way they really are?

- *Beloved... abstain from fleshly lusts which war against the soul (1 Peter 2:11, NKJ).*

  Are you guilty of a lustful eye toward the opposite sex? Do you fill your mind with sex-oriented TV programs, movies, books, magazines? Their covers? Centerfolds? Do you indulge in any lustful activity that God's Word condemns—fornication, adultery, perversion?

- *By this all will know that you are My disciples, if you have love for one another (John 13:35, NKJ).*

  Are you guilty of being a part of factions and divisions in your church? Would you rather add fuel to a misunderstanding than help correct it? Have you loved only the ones in your own church, feeling those of other denominations are not of the body of Christ? Are you secretly pleased over the misfortunes of another? Annoyed by their successes?

- *Bearing with one another, and forgiving one another, if anyone has a complaint against another; even as Christ forgave you, so you also must do (Colossians 3:13, NKJ).*

Have you failed to forgive anybody anything they might have said or done against you? Have you turned certain people off? Are you holding grudges?

■ *Let him who stole steal no longer, but rather let him labor (Ephesians 4:28, NKJ).*

Do you steal from your employer by doing less work, staying on the job less time than you are paid for? Do you "pad" your expense account?

■ *No one can serve two masters ... You cannot serve God and [money] (Matthew 6:24, NKJ).*

Is your goal in life to make as much money as possible? Accumulate things? Have you withheld God's share of your income from Him? Is money your God?

■ *You outwardly appear righteous to men, but inside you are full of hypocrisy and lawlessness (Matthew 23:28, NKJ).*

Do you know in your heart that you are a fake, just pretending to be a real Christian? Are you hiding behind church membership to cover a life still full of sin? Are you faking Christianity for social status, acceptance in your church, community? Do you smile piously during the Sunday sermon but live in your sin all week? Are you the person in your home that you are trying to impress people you are?

■ *Finally, brethren, whatever things are true, whatever things are noble, whatever things are just, whatever things are pure, whatever things are lovely, whatever things are of good report, if there is any virtue and if there is anything praiseworthy— meditate on these things (Philippians 4:8, NKJ).*

Do you enjoy listening to gossip? Passing it on? Do you believe rumors or partial truths, especially about an enemy or your competitor? Do you fail to spend time every day reading the Bible? Do you fail to think on the things of God—only good and true and pure things—always?

Now make your list on the basis of the above questions and whatever else God has said to you. Claim the promise of 1 John 1:9. When you have confessed your sins before God, acknowledge that He has forgiven you through Christ's death on the cross (Hebrews 10:1–23).

Then you repent, which means that you change your attitude toward sin. The power of the Holy Spirit will enable you to change both your attitude and conduct. Instead of doing what your old sinful nature—your flesh—wants to do, choose to do what God wants you to do.

You inhale by appropriating the fullness of God's Spirit by faith. Trust Him to control and empower you according to His command in Ephesians 5:18 to "be filled with the Spirit." This actually means to be constantly and continually controlled and empowered with the Holy Spirit.

According to His *promise* in 1 John 5:14,15, God hears you and grants your request because you pray according to His will.

> This is the confidence we have in approaching God: that if we ask anything according to his will, he hears us. And if we know that he hears us—whatever we ask—we know that we have what we asked of him.

The average Christian does not understand that Spiritual Breathing is an exercise of faith. As a result, he lives on a spiritual roller coaster. He goes from one emotional experience to another living most of his life as a worldly Christian, controlling his own life—frustrated and fruitless.

If this is your experience, Spiritual Breathing will enable you to get off this emotional roller coaster and to enjoy the abundant Christian life that the Lord Jesus promised to you when He said, "I have come that they may have life, and that they may have it more abundantly" (John 10:10, NKJ). Spiritual Breathing also will make it possible for you to continue to experience God's love, forgiveness, and the power and control of the Holy Spirit as a way of life.

The moment you invited Christ into your life as Savior and Lord, you experienced a spiritual rebirth. You became a child of God and you were filled with the Holy Spirit. God forgave your sins—past, present, and future—making you righteous, holy, and acceptable in His sight because of Christ's sacrifice for you on the cross. You were given the power to live a holy life and to be a fruitful witness for God. As you walk in the Spirit by faith, practicing Spiritual Breathing, you need never live in spiritual defeat.

Making Physical Preparations

The third step in getting ready to fast is to *prepare yourself physically.*

Do not rush into a fast. If you plan to go without food for several days, you will find it helpful to begin by eating smaller meals before you abstain altogether. This sends your mind a signal that you have entered the time of the fast, and it helps to "shrink" your stomach and appetite. (Of course, if you are taking prescription medications, be sure to consult your doctor.)

Lee Bueno, a strong advocate of preparing ourselves, says:

> Because many people experience a great drop in their blood sugar when they forsake their usual high-fat, high-sugar diets, you may want to wean yourself from these foods a day or two before your fast.[2]

Some health professionals suggest eating only raw foods for two days before starting a fast.[3]

Preparing yourself physically makes the drastic change in your eating routine a little easier. Then you can turn your full attention to the Lord in prayer.

Fourth, *ask the Holy Spirit to reveal the kind of fast God wants you to undertake.* Does He want you to go completely without food, consuming only water? Or water and juices? Is He asking you to fast one meal a day, one day a week, or several days or weeks at a time? Is God leading you to undertake a forty-day fast? Inviting the Holy Spirit's guidance in this matter will make your time with God more meaningful.

Token fasting, such as giving up chocolates or lemon pie or some other favorite food, may be commendable, but this does not allow the Holy Spirit to do the inner work necessary to bring about real changes in your spiritual life. Nor does it persuade God that you are serious about revival for America.

As I pointed out earlier, the biblical fast usually calls for water. I have conducted many strictly water fasts for a day or several days at a time with special blessing. However, I strongly suggest adding vegetable and fruit juices to your intake.

Because of their acid content, nutritionist Dr. James F. Balch does not advise orange or tomato juice. The best juices, he believes, are fresh cabbage, beet, carrot, celery, grape, and apple. He also recommends "green drinks" made from green leafy vegetables because they are excellent detoxifiers.[4] If you choose to follow a water-only fast, please do so under the guidelines of a medical doctor trained in how to fast.

Like Dr. Balch, nutritionist Pamela Smith advises against citrus juices due to the citric acid. She suggests "soft" juices like unsweetened apple, apple-cranberry, or white grape juice.[5]

I recommend fruit juices for two reasons: their natural sugars provide energy, and the taste and the strength are motivational to continue your fast.

Dr. Balch says fruit juices are cleansers and are best taken in the morning. Since vegetable juices are restorers and builders, they are best taken in the afternoon.[6]

A combination distilled water and juice fast is very wise—especially for those who are new to fasting—because it helps them concentrate more on the Lord than on their hunger pains and possible discomfort or feelings of sickness that sometimes accompany a water-only fast.

Once you know how to fast, short fasts of one to three days require no more than water. Christians who fast regularly often go ten days or longer on water—even up to forty days—with beneficial effects, both spiritually and physically, under the daily supervision of one who is knowledgeable about water fasting. You have more food reserves stored in body fat than you realize, and most of us would be more than happy to give up the fat.[7]

However, until you build up your "fasting muscles," or if you are undertaking a long fast, you may want to add vegetable or fruit juices (preferably without sugar or sweeteners) to your intake.

Dr. Julio Ruibal believes a person can comfortably fast on juices for as long as he feels God is leading him to do so. He recommends juice intake beginning with the third day. "On a juice fast, your body takes in certain nutrients," Dr. Ruibal says. "Fruit juices provide glucose. Watermelon is excellent because it is basically water with glucose. It is mild and non-reactive. Just put it in the blender without adding water. Juice made from fresh apples also is good. A green juice made from celery, romaine lettuce, and carrots blended in more or less equal proportions provides the minerals that your body needs for many of its nerve functions. This will enable you to engage in some degree of productive activity."

Nutritionists recommend that you avoid caffeine beverages such as coffee, tea, or cola. "The caffeine, sulfuric acids, and phosphorous in these drinks are not good for the body. In fact, they are dangerous," Dr. Ruibal says. Because caffeine is a stimulant, it has a more powerful effect on your nervous system when you abstain from food. This works against both the physical and spiritual benefits of the fast.

"When you feel hunger pains due to the absence of stimulants, just increase your liquid intake," Dr. Ruibal says. "Herb teas are permissible, but take it easy on the honey."

For colder climates, Dr. Ruibal recommends warm broth. Simply boil sliced potatoes, carrots, and celery in water. Do not add salt. After about a half hour, drain off the water and drink it. This also gives variety of taste in liquids.

Dr. Balch suggests another recipe for broth:

> Three carrots, two stalks of celery, one turnip, two beets, a half head of cabbage, a quarter of a bunch of parsley, a quarter of an onion, and a half clove of garlic.[8]

He recommends boiling the vegetables gently, then drinking the broth two to three times a day.

Dr. Ruibal suggests a daily schedule that you may find useful during your fast:

5 a.m. — 8 a.m.

Fruit juices, preferably freshly squeezed or blended and diluted in 50 percent distilled water if the fruit is acid. Orange, apple, pear, grapefruit, papaya, or other fruit are good. If you are unable to prepare your juices, buy juices without sugar or additives.

10:30 a.m. — noon

Green vegetable juice freshly made from lettuce, celery, and carrots in three equal parts.

2:30 p.m. — 4 p.m.

Herb tea with a drop of honey. Make sure that it is not black tea or tea with a stimulant.

6 p.m. — 8:30 p.m.

Broth made from boiling potatoes, celery, and carrots with no salt. After boiling about half an hour, pour the water into a container and drink it.

I suggest that you do not drink milk because it is a pure food and therefore a violation of the fast.

You may drink as much water as you like. The body needs plenty of water on a fast—both to cleanse the system and to prevent dehydration. For easy access, you may want to keep a small bottle of distilled water by your side. Drinking water at mealtime "fools" your stomach and makes it stop "talking" because it thinks it is being fed.

If you do not wish to follow Dr. Ruibal's recommended schedule, you may drink vegetable and fruit juices throughout the day. But exercise self-control. Remember, you are on a spiritual fast. If you do not discipline your quantity of juice consumption, you may defeat your spiritual purpose.

A further word of counsel is offered by Dr. Balch:

> Do not chew anything, such as gum, while on the fast. The digestive process starts with chewing—enzymes are secreted into the gastrointestinal tract. With no food in the stomach for these enzymes to digest, trouble occurs.[9]

Fifth, *limit your activity level*. Exercise only moderately. Rest as much as your schedule will permit. Short naps are very helpful. "Resting is not a sin," Dr. Ruibal explains. "Fasting in the strictest sense is physiological rest. Your body rests from the processes involved in digestion and the assimilation of food to concentrate on excretion."

That is why during the fast you may experience side effects. "Many experience headaches, stomach aches, nausea, foul tastes in their mouth, or a pasty tongue," Dr. Ruibal says. "Their urine may become darker, and even their sweat may smell worse than usual. Vomiting may occur. This is normal. In a prolonged fast, it is not unusual to experience a fever. Basically, the body is taking advantage of the fast to clean and heal itself."

Sixth, *consider your medications*. It is particularly important that you consult with your doctor before going on a fast if you are on any prescribed medication. "You could run into physical problems when you are on a fast and continue with the medication," Dr. Ruibal warns.

"Most people can be liberated from medications for high blood pressure when they follow the proper diet, exercise, and stress management," he says. "But you must be very careful. Have your blood pressure checked regularly and, if you see that you need your medication, begin taking it again."[10] Any changes in taking your medication should be done with your doctor's approval and under his supervision.

Planning Your Prayer Time

The seventh step in conducting a fast is to *set aside ample time to be alone with the Lord*. The more time you spend with Him in fellowship, worship, and adoration, the more you read and meditate upon His Word during your fast, the greater your effectiveness will be in prayer and the more meaningful your fast.

Seek God in prayer and as you meditate on His Word each morning before you leave home or go about your daily routine. Return to prayer at lunch, and come before Him again in the evening for unhurried times of "seeking His face." Of course, you should "practice His presence" and continue to have fellowship with Him constantly as you "pray without ceasing" throughout the day.

There is no set formula for how to pray when you fast. You may wish to pray aloud or silently, asking the Lord to grant specific requests. I suggest that you make a list and add to it daily as needs come to mind. Pray earnestly for your family, your pastor, your church, your community, and our nation.

> *"I, a mortal man, can speak to the Sovereign of the universe and He will answer me. Then I realized: Adrian, you're a fool because you don't pray more than you do."*
>
> —*Dr. Adrian Rogers, pastor*
> *Bellevue Baptist Church*
> *Memphis*

Pray for revival in our land and a great worldwide spiritual harvest. Pray for the fulfillment of the Great Commission.

You may wait before Him in quiet meditation as you invite the Holy Spirit to minister to you and bring to mind those things He wants you to pray about.

You should go about your daily activities mindful that you are still fasting and seeking the Lord. Some of my deepest spiritual insights have come as I continued my ministry responsibilities while "seeking His face" and "practicing His presence."

If you do not know what to pray for, or you feel "prayed out," wait quietly before Him. Turn to the Psalms or other favorite passages of Scripture and pray the Word of God back to Him. For example, read Psalm 23 and then pray each verse aloud, thanking Him for performing each of those promises in your life. Worship and praise the Lord. Tell God how much you love Him and want to serve Him. Invite His presence into your life in a fresh way.

You may wish to approach God with the Lord's Prayer recorded in Matthew 6:9–13. Generally, this prayer covers everything we could possibly ask or say to God. As an introduction to this prayer, Jesus reminded His disciples that "your Father knows what you need before you ask him" (Matthew 6:8).

Now that you have an idea of how to go about fasting, it is time to fix your gaze upon the One who sees you and knows you—the One who delights in you and is waiting for you to come before Him.

CHAPTER 10

Beginning Your Fast

Your time for fasting and prayer has come. You are abstaining from all solid foods and have begun to seek the Lord. Oddly enough, this is the very moment when some sense a little letdown—an uneasy feeling that says, "Well, here I am. Now what do I do?

If you are one of those who measure spiritual success by your emotions or by how much you visibly achieve, this can be a period when you may feel somewhat confused. If that happens you must exercise resolve and patience, relax in the Lord and invite the Holy Spirit to help you. As you seek the Lord in faith, you can be assured that He will enable you to complete the fast that He has called you to begin.

Permit me to share some helpful suggestions to consider while you are fasting.

First, *restrict your activity.* Rigorous exercise such as cycling, fast walking, and jogging come highly recommended with programs that offer special diets for health and weight loss—but not for fasting.

Walking a mile or two each day at a moderate pace can be healthful for a person in good health while strictly on a juice fast. However, no one on a water fast should exercise without the supervision of a fasting specialist.[1]

If you engage in strenuous labor, you may want to fast only one day during the week, limiting yourself to partial fasting. Or you may look to weekends as the prime time to abstain from food.

Second, *expect to visit the "facilities" often.* Drinking plenty of fluids will necessitate this. You may wish to take enemas or laxatives before, during, and after your fast. Nutritionists who teach fasting disagree over whether you need to do this. They do agree, however, that once you stop eating, your bowels cease normal functions. And, once you start eating again, the digestive tract resumes its normal movements. If you decide on an extended fast, you may want to investigate this matter further to your own satisfaction.[2]

During my forty-day fast, I drank psyllium, which can be purchased in most drug and health food stores. Mixed in water, psyllium powder becomes like jello. It provided the fiber I needed to help cleanse my system.

Third, *be prepared for mental discomforts.* You will experience some inner conflict when you deny yourself the pleasure of eating delicious food. During a three-day fast, this struggle can intensify toward the end of the second day. That seems to be a favorite time for the "self" to rise up and say, "Hey, this is as far as I want to go. Haven't we done enough?"

> *Fasting requires reasonable precautions.*

You may feel impatient and irritable. It is not unusual for one to become cranky and anxious during a protracted fast. Vonette, who fasted with me for the last fourteen days of my fast, experienced some of those feelings.

You can also expect the enemy to oppose you—whispering thoughts that test your resolve. When this happens to you, invite the Lord to cleanse your mind with His blood and empower you with His Holy Spirit.

Fourth, *expect physical discomforts.* You may experience a case of the physical "blahs" during the first few days. If so, sip water and juices frequently, and rest while seeking strength in prayer, worship, and God's Word.

By the end of the second day, you may discover that you are very hungry—in your stomach and in your mind—but by the end of the third day, you may no longer feel hungry. However, you may feel a little weak.

Hunger and weakness are variables. Bueno says:

> After the first two or three days, hunger leaves... [and] the *craving* for food disappears. Remember that appetite is a mental desire; hunger is a bodily need.[3]

You would think that the longer you fast the weaker you would become. But healthy persons report that during extended fasts they actually experience a new vitality. As the body cleanses itself of toxins and begins to feed off of its reserves, the stomach stops demanding food and there is often a sense of physical well-being.[4] I truly felt better during my long fast than when I was eating normally.

Some physical discomforts can be traced to withdrawal from a diet that includes refined sugar and caffeine found in coffee, tea, or most carbonated drinks. Since I have never drunk coffee and very little tea or colas, I did not have a problem with headaches, dizziness, or any other difficulties in completing my forty-day fast.

After fasting several days, dizziness may be caused by a sudden change in position, such as rising suddenly from a chair. To remedy this, stop for a second or two, recover, and remember to move slowly. Headaches or mild dizziness could also be caused by the accumulation of toxins in your colon. (*A word of caution:* These conditions could be symptoms of other problems requiring medical attention.) Doctors recommend a tablespoon of psyllium powder morning and evening to hasten the elimination of toxins from your colon and help to prevent headaches and dizziness for most healthy people.

Sleeplessness and an overactive mind frequently accompany a fast due to toxins in the blood stream. Prayer, meditating in the Word, and a nice slow walk around the block should help.[5]

You may experience some weight loss, especially during an extended fast. But do not worry; you will very likely gain it all back! Nutritionist Pamela Smith says: "Your metabolism has greatly slowed in response to no food and will quickly store large amounts of food taken in after the fast. This is why any weight loss in fasting is quickly [restored]."[6]

No two fasts will be exactly alike. You may experience some struggles during one fast that do not appear the next time. The degree of difficulty you may experience seems to depend on your spiritual and physical condition at the time.

How Long Should I Fast?

The New Testament offers no detailed guidance on how long to go without food for spiritual purposes. If you have never fasted, I encourage you to start slowly. As you learn what to expect, begin to increase the length of your fast. Try going without a meal or two first, then build up to 24-hour fasts, then two days, three days, and so on.[7] The rule of thumb is not to give up in the middle of an emotional battle over food and to give the Holy Spirit time to carry out His inner work in you.

God's Word often mentions three-day fasts. You may wish to enter longer fasts—five to ten days—but only after you are more experienced with fasting. The Holy Spirit has clearly impressed me to pray for two million Christians to fast a full forty days for the coming revival.

Remember, God understands your situation. His wisdom is infinite. He wants you to *learn* to fast. If you know little about fasting but feel "led" to start an extended fast, you may be listening to someone other than the Holy Spirit. He will not lead you to do anything that may cause you physical problems and damage your faith in Him.

For long fasts, choosing the proper time to do it is especially important. Searching for the best opportunity to undertake my forty-day fast, I had to make several adjustments in my work schedule. You may be able to fast for an extended period without any significant interruption in your work habits or lifestyle. But do not wait for an ideal time. When the Holy Spirit touches your heart, you can fast any time He leads you to do so. If your life is as busy as most people, you may never get around to fasting if you wait for "the right time."

Lee Bueno counsels, "A short fast of one to three days can be taken virtually any time. Fasting from Friday to Monday morning would give you the entire weekend to rest and spend time reading Scripture. Another ideal time to fast is during vacations from work."[8]

I do not recommend fasting during the Thanksgiving and Christmas holidays. Those are special times for family, food, and fellowship, and fasting at these times may prove to be difficult for you and an inconvenience to your loved ones.

May I Tell Others About My Fast?

Jesus gave His instructions for prayer and fasting in Matthew 6:

> And when you pray, do not be like the hypocrites, for they love to pray standing in the synagogues and on the street corners to be seen by men. I tell you the truth, they have received their reward in full. But when you pray, go into your room, close the door and pray to your Father, who is unseen. Then your Father, who sees what is done in secret, will reward you. And when you pray, do not keep on babbling like pagans, for they think they will be heard because of their many words. Do not be like them, for your Father knows what you need before you ask him (6:5–9).

> When you fast, do not look somber as the hypocrites do, for they disfigure their faces to show men they are fasting. I tell you the truth, they have received their reward in full. But when you fast, put oil on your head and wash your face, so that it will not be obvious to men

that you are fasting, but only to your Father, who is unseen; and your Father, who sees what is done in secret, will reward you (6:16–18).

Some interpret this passage to mean that it is wrong to let others know we are fasting. But Jesus was dealing with the hypocrisy of the Pharisees who made prayer and fasting a point of ritual and boasting to demonstrate their piety.

In this passage, Jesus is not forbidding us to tell others of our fasting. Rather, He is saying, "Avoid boasting and acting superior to others. Fasting is not an occasion to demonstrate your spirituality or to gain glory for yourself."

Let me emphasize again, fasting does not make us spiritually elite. Rather, it creates in us a sense of humility. In fasting, the first thing one does is humble himself before God. If we are fasting with a pure heart, our occasion to tell others will demonstrate a humble attitude. The very thought of exalting ourselves will be abhorrent.

I believe that fasting in secret for the sake of secrecy is a lie of the enemy. Satan does not want us to fast. He has kept it from most of the Church all these years. One wonders how he succeeded because it is so important to vital Christianity.

Since fasting with prayer is one of the most powerful tools in the hands of believers, Christians should have the freedom to fast openly. How else can they be mentors of this spiritual discipline to weak Christians? How can they promote fasting on a large scale, such as when hundreds of America's top leaders gathered in Orlando for three days of fasting and prayer for our country? How can they participate in a church-wide fast and keep it quiet?

If we limited our prayers to the "closet," we would have no church prayer meetings. I want to encourage believers to fast and pray together in large numbers in their churches so they will be an inspiration to others.

Fasting outwardly as a testimony of our faith and love for Christ and our desire to please Him is commendable. We only displease the Lord and lose our blessing when we fast to be seen of men as did the Pharisees.

As you fast, carefully select those whom you tell. Some people may try to discourage you. Never expect encouragement from those who do not fast. One of the most demoralizing things that can happen to you is when friends or family disapprove. It can be particularly disheartening when your doctor or pastor frowns on the idea. Before beginning my forty-day fast, I received no encouragement from anyone. And several friends registered grave concern for my health and well-being.

In selecting the time to fast, you may need to discuss it with those with whom you live—your spouse, parents, or roommate. They have a right to know, and you may need their cooperation. You may also need to tell your supervisor or others at work if they ask you to join them for lunch.

How to Break Your Fast
When your designated time of fasting is finished, you will begin to eat again. But how you break your fast is extremely important—both for your physical and spiritual well-being.

If you end your fast gradually, as you should, the beneficial physical and spiritual effects will linger for days. But if you rush into eating solid foods—and the prospect of food can cause you to do that—you may experience diarrhea, sickness, fainting, and even death due to shock. This is especially true of an extended fast. Nutritionist Paul Bragg explains:

> When you have been on a...fast, your stomach and the thirty feet of intestinal tract have contracted, and when you are ready to break the fast, it should be done [with special care].[9]

Suddenly reintroducing solid food to your stomach and digestive tract always creates defeating effects. You can lose much of your deep sense of peace and well-being in the space of a single meal. Pamela Smith encourages you to "wisely break the fast—not with a huge meal or feeding frenzy..."[10]

Dr. Julio Ruibal advises coming out of an extended water fast with fruit. "The best is watermelon," he says. "Oranges need to be diluted because of the acids." For a juice fast, he offers the following suggestions:

> A juice fast should be ended with a raw salad for the first day. The second day you may add to your raw salad a baked or boiled potato. Do not add salt, butter, or any other seasoning. The third day, add a steamed vegetable to your salad and potato. Then you may begin to reintroduce your normal diet.

Dr. Ruibal cautions against overeating after your fast. "Don't gorge yourself. You can literally kill yourself that way," he warns. "You could tie up your intestines so badly that you may need to be hospitalized."[11]

Even a three-day fast requires reasonable precautions. It is wise to start with a little soup—something thin and nourishing such as vegetable broth made from onion, celery, potatoes, and carrots—and fresh fruits such as watermelon and cantaloupe.

As your body accepts these foods, advance to a few tablespoons of solid foods such as raw fruits and vegetables or a raw salad and baked potato. (I do not recommend milk or milk products and meat because some individuals may suffer adverse reactions to these after a fast.) Then, several hours later, try another small snack. The idea is to ease back into regular eating with several small snacks during the first few days. This requires discipline, but you will avoid the severe pain and other serious physical reactions that come from eating too much too soon.[12]

I terminated my forty-day fast with a cup of soup, followed by small amounts of watermelon and other fruits every few hours for a couple of days until I was comfortable with resuming my normal routine of eating. As you can imagine, that cup of soup and first few bites of solid food were ecstasy. Never had ordinary food tasted so good. (Remember, doctors urge us not to resume eating with a large, hearty meal after a long fast; that could be dangerous.)

Overcoming Failure

Every fast has its struggles, discomforts, spiritual victories, and failures. In the morning you may feel like you are on top of the world, but by evening you may be wrestling with the flesh—sorely tempted to raid the refrigerator and counting how much longer you have to go. This is especially true if you are new at fasting. Take time to step outside for some fresh air and a moderate walk of a mile or two.

If you fail to make it through your first fast, do not be discouraged. Quitting a fast may only mean that you may have tried to fast too long the first time out, or that you need to strengthen your understanding and resolve. As soon as possible, undertake another fast until you do succeed.

Expect a Change in You

No two persons will experience the same effects of a fast because no two persons go into it in exactly the same condition or with the same needs. But if you sincerely humble yourself before the Lord in repentance, intercession, and worship, and consistently meditate on His Word, you will experience a heightened awareness of His presence. Your confidence and faith in God will be strengthened. And you will feel mentally, spiritually, and physically refreshed. My fast proved to be the greatest prolonged spiritual blessing of my life.

Most people experience a measure of revival as a result of fasting. But just as we need fresh infillings of the Holy Spirit daily, we also need new times of fasting before God. A single fast is not a spiritual cure-all. John and Charles Wesley advocated fasting two days a week to "keep the flesh under" and to maintain the closeness with God that fasting brings.

I encourage you to join me in fasting and prayer again and again and again until we truly experience revival in our homes, our churches, our beloved nation, and in the world.

CHAPTER 11

America at the Crossroads

In my fifty years of walking with the Lord, I have never witnessed a greater concern for the spiritual condition of this nation. Everywhere, concerned citizens—especially Christians—are deeply troubled over the wicked things that are happening in our country.

As a nation, we live in the most critical moment in our history. From a human standpoint, there is no way out of this moral morass. Not one of our institutions—government, education, judicial, science, business, media, military, the Church, or the home—offers a ray of hope.

As individual Christians and as a Church, we are prone to be so comfortable, so materialistic, so indifferent to spiritual discipline, so racked by scandals and loss of respect that secular society sees little difference between believers and the rest of the world.

Most believers have lost their sense of a holy God, and the reality of God has little effect on their everyday life. Unless God does something to bring revival, American believers will go down with the national ship.

Indeed, our future looks bleak. The words of President Abraham Lincoln are even more true today than they were on April 30, 1863, when he proclaimed a National Day of Fasting, Humiliation, and Prayer.

> We have been the recipients of the choicest bounties of heaven. We have been preserved, these many years, in peace and prosperity. We have grown in numbers, wealth and power, as no other nation has ever grown.

But we have forgotten God. We have forgotten the gracious hand which preserved us in peace, and multiplied and enriched and strengthened us; and we have vainly imagined, in the deceitfulness of our hearts, that all these blessings were produced by some superior wisdom and virtue of our own. Intoxicated with unbroken success, we have become too self-sufficient to feel the necessity of redeeming and preserving grace, too proud to pray to the God that made us! It behooves us, then, to humble ourselves before the offended Power, to confess our national sins, and to pray for clemency and forgiveness.

America was then, and is today, at a crossroads. In the words of author John Price, "The destruction of Nineveh could easily fit the United States today."[1]

God Wants Revival

I believe God wants to spare our nation and am confident that He is going to send a great spiritual awakening to America and the world. God is touching the hearts of many influential Christians across our land, as He has touched mine. He is convicting His people—persuading them of their sin and the sins of the country—in preparation for the coming revival.

In his book *The Turning Tide,* Pat Robertson declares that the time is ripe for drastic change. He says the hearts of the people are yearning for a return to the values that made America great. Robertson writes:

> We have come to an unprecedented moment in our history—a time when the potential for positive change has never been greater. In the midst of political turmoil and discontent, we are seeing a renewal—a reawakening of the personal values and beliefs that have sustained this nation throughout its history.[2]

Addressing more than six hundred of our nation's Christian leaders during the special days of fasting and prayer in Orlando, Robertson said, "God is visiting the earth. I have never seen such response to the gospel as I see these days. This is an unbelievable time of [spiritual] hunger in the world."

David McKenna, author of *The Coming Great Awakening*, sees certain stirrings on college campuses that he believes will result in a revival by the year 2000.[3]

Few seem able to grasp how easy it will be for the revival fire of God to sweep around the world, but past revivals show how powerful our Lord really is.

The Lord ignited the New England colonies in the mid 1700s, for example, with the powerful, soul-searching sermons of Jonathan Edwards on repentance. George Whitefield joined Edwards in this preaching, and so many sinners were converted that the course of the nation was changed. And, as we have seen, the 1904 Welsh revival spread to England and the continents, spanning the oceans to America where twenty million came to Christ.

During my forty-day fast, the Holy Spirit assured me again and again that God will send a great revival to America and the world when His people heed His call to turn to Him, according to 2 Chronicles 7:14. I am confident that this awakening will result in the greatest spiritual harvest in history, and the Great Commission will be fulfilled in our generation.

What the Revival Will Do

If awakenings of the past foreshadow events to come, I believe we will see the fire of the Holy Spirit break out in the churches and spread to every nook and cranny in the land. We will see revival begin with God's people, but millions of unbelievers everywhere—in government, education, the media, Hollywood—will turn to Christ in unprecedented numbers. That is the nature of true revival. It is never contained within church walls.

As this revival sweeps throughout our nation and around the world, we will see renewed religious fervor. There will be a fresh awareness of the awesomeness of God and His other attributes, a restoration of true worship, a hunger for the Word of God, and a new zeal to help fulfill the Great Commission, telling others about our Lord Jesus Christ and the good news of God's love and forgiveness. (In fact, if revival does not result in massive evangelization, it is not a true awakening.) We also will see a renewed vision for social issues and racial reconciliation.

When revival comes, Christians will exercise greater influence in their communities and in our nation. As a result of fasting and prayer and personal revival, they will:

- Demonstrate the supernatural love of God in their personal lives, their homes, their churches, and in all of their secular relationships.

- Become actively involved in restoring every facet of society, including government, to the biblical values of our Founding Fathers.

- Cease supporting the immorality-makers by avoiding movies, home videos, and television programs that patronize lust and sex, and return to the basic Bible values of our founding fathers.

- Influence the media by encouraging secular editors and broadcasters to present a fair and balanced view of the religious community.

- Support Christian organizations committed to restoring our vital freedoms.

- Help their politicians know what they stand for and seek to put in public office those who live upright lives and fight for moral causes.

- Work harder to restore godly standards for right and wrong in our educational system.

How the Revival Will Come

Such revival comes as a sovereign act of God—as the result of Christian people meeting God's conditions by responding to the work of the Holy Spirit.

I believe three things must happen before this revival can take place:

First, *Christian leaders must catch the vision.* They must play a prominent role in presenting the call of the Holy Spirit to their congregations. I believe it is the duty of pastors to lead their people to repentance—by personal example as well as by proclamation. Joel records:

> O ministers of my God, lie all night before the altar, weeping…Announce a fast; call a solemn meeting. Gather the elders and all the people into the Temple of the Lord your God, and weep before him there.
>
> Alas, this terrible day of punishment is on the way. Destruction from the Almighty is almost here! (Joel 1:13–15, TLB).

We need dedicated ministers of God who are not afraid to call their people to repentance—even if this results in great personal sacrifice. Jonathan Edwards, for example, lost his pulpit when he put out his fiery call to repentance.

But other Christian leaders must also take up the banner. Broadcasters, heads of parachurch organizations, evangelists, and influential lay leaders must all herald God's call.

Second, *God's people must heed the call to repentance, fasting, and prayer.* As I have said, the promise of the coming revival carries one condition. Before God lifts His present hand of judgment from America, believers by the millions must first humble themselves and seek His face in fasting and prayer, according to 2 Chronicles 7:14:

> If my people, who are called by my name, will humble themselves and pray and seek my face and turn from their wicked ways, then I will hear from heaven and will forgive their sin and will heal their land.

Since fasting is a biblical means of humbling ourselves, it is the only spiritual discipline that enables us to meet all the conditions of this passage.   *Ezra 8:21; Ps 35:13*

God's prerequisite is not an option. Throughout His Word, God clearly says: "If you obey Me, I will bless you; if you disobey Me, I will discipline you; and if you continue to disobey Me, I will destroy you." This occurred repeatedly in the life of Israel. When Abraham interceded for Sodom, the Lord promised He would spare the wicked city if He could find at least ten righteous persons there (Genesis 18:32). But God could not find ten righteous in the city. Only Lot and his family were spared as they fled the holocaust. We should take this as a warning.

If we could peer over the balcony of time into our future, would we view a similar scene? As we have noted, America is under moral and spiritual siege. An avalanche of judgments has fallen upon this country because America is rapidly becoming a godless society. The spirit of anti-Christ rules nearly every public institution. We are no longer "one nation under God, indivisible, with liberty and justice for all."

I believe the wickedness now overwhelming America qualifies as judgments of God, and—if left unchecked—these judgments will destroy us. England, once the bastian of Christian faith and practice and the most missionary nation on earth, now stretches to find true believers among a very small segment of its population.[4]

God is calling His people to revival. His Word in Joel 2:12,13 applies today as it did in the prophet's time:

> "Even now," declares the Lord, "return to me with all your heart, with fasting and weeping and mourning."
> Rend your heart and not your garments. Return to the Lord your God, for he is gracious and compassionate, slow to anger and abounding in love, and he relents from sending calamity.

In Isaiah 30:21 God said, "Whether you turn to the right or to the left, your ears will hear a voice behind you saying, 'This is the way; walk in it.'" The call to repentance, fasting, and prayer is clearly distinguishable to all who will listen.

No one needs to wait for a leader or until revival breaks out across the land to experience personal renewal. God will send an awakening to this nation as His people, one by one, obey His call and yield themselves to the Spirit of God. Jesus said, "Blessed are those who hunger and thirst for righteousness, for *they* will be filled" (Matthew 5:6).

The story of what happened in a youth camp in Southern California is only one of many thousands of examples that illustrate God's response to our repentance and prayer. After a season of heart-broken prayer by camp leaders, the Holy Spirit moved among the young people in a mighty way during an evening meeting.

Scores wept because of their sin; some received assurance of salvation; other nonbelievers received Christ into their lives; many reconciled their differences with each other; and others surrendered to full-time Christian service.

The meeting lasted late into the night as the Holy Spirit continued to move in their midst. Both the young people and the leaders experienced new vitality in their spiritual lives because of this revival.

Third, *the Holy Spirit must convict the nation of its sins.* No revival is possible without the convicting power of the Holy Spirit. Jesus said, "When [the Holy Spirit] comes, he will convict the world of guilt in regard to sin and righteousness and judgment" (John 16:8). As Christians humble themselves before the Lord, the Holy Spirit will convict people of their sins, cause them to repent, bring healing to His people, and restore blessing to our land.

What You Must Do

Let me share with you several steps that will help you prepare for your personal revival and experience more fully the presence and power of the Holy Spirit in your life.

First, *ask the Holy Spirit to reveal any unconfessed sin in your life.* Is there bitterness, unbelief, or unforgiveness? Are you spiritually cold, having left your first love of the Lord? Have you lost your love of meditating on His Word? Have your schedule and personal affairs come between you and your Savior? Do you still want to please God above all else? Have you lost your willingness to sacrifice your time, comforts, pleasures, and even your reputation to see God move in your life and in your church?

Spiritual preparation through repentance is vital for revival. "Righteousness," said the psalmist, "goes before him and prepares the way for his steps" (Psalm 85:13).

> "*I am deeply aware of a coming revival. The water is building up behind the dam. I think fasting is a vehicle of revival.*"
>
> —Dr. Mark Rutland, pastor
> Calvary Assembly of God
> Winter Park, Florida

"Answered prayer does not come to those whose hands are dirty," Pat Robertson says. "If God answers those who knowingly live in sin, He gives them the message that He condones their sinful lifestyle. We need to stop making excuses and repent of our sins as soon as we come into His presence."[5] Confessing your sin—with a willingness to forsake it and surrender your will to God—frees the Holy Spirit to activate His power and work through you.

Second, *be filled with the Holy Spirit.* If you are a Christian, God in the person of the Father, Son, and Holy Spirit is already living within you. Great spiritual power and resources are available to you. To be filled with the Spirit, trust

Him to control and empower you according to His *command* and *promise.*

In Ephesians 5:18, we are *commanded:*

> Do not get drunk on wine, which leads to debauchery. Instead, be filled with the Spirit.

And in 1 John 5:14,15, we are *promised:*

> This is the confidence we have in approaching God: that if we ask anything according to his will, he hears us. And if we know that He hears us—whatever we ask—we know that we have what we asked of him.

Expect to be filled. We know that it is God's will that every believer be filled with His Spirit. Therefore, as we invite the Holy Spirit to fill us, we can know according to the Word of God that our prayer will be answered.

I encourage you to find a quiet place where you can be alone with God. You do not have to wait for a special move of the Holy Spirit. He is waiting for you to invite Him to fill you now.

Third, *seek to live in God's presence as a way of life.* This is more than just being aware that He is always with you. Luke records in the Book of Acts: "In him we live and move and have our being" (Acts 17:28). Living in God's presence means that you find your total existence in Him. God becomes the motivation and purpose of every activity of your life—family, business, social, and spiritual. You do not ask Him to work for you, you ask Him to work through you.

Fourth, *love with God's love.* Jesus wept with compassion over the spiritual condition of those He came to save. We usually care more deeply about our own friends and loved ones, yet there are many individuals who weep in genuine concern for all of humanity. Loving with God's love means we allow our hearts to be broken for the lost, as was the heart of Jesus.

As you humble yourself before the Lord in fasting and prayer, ask Him to fill you with His love; ask Him to give you a deep burden for the lost in our nation.

Our Lord commands us to love. He said:

> "Love the Lord your God with all your heart, soul, and mind." This is the first and greatest commandment. The second most important is similar: "Love your neighbor as much as you love yourself." All the other commandments and all the demands of the prophets stem from these two laws and are fulfilled if you obey them. Keep only these and you will find that you are obeying all the others (Matthew 22:37–40, TLB).

Sometimes you may find it difficult to love. But you can love by *faith*. In 1 John 5:14,15, God promises that if you ask anything according to His will, He hears and answers you. Relating this promise to God's command to love, you can claim by faith the privilege of loving with His love. Everything about the Christian life is based on faith. You love by faith just as you received Christ by faith, just as you are filled with the Holy Spirit by faith, and just as you walk by faith.

God has an unending supply of His divine, supernatural, *agape* love for you. In order to experience and share this love, you must claim it by faith; that is, trust His promise that He will give you all that you need to do His will on the basis of His *command* and *promise*.

Fifth, *seek God diligently*. God's work in the hearts of people is accomplished through the power of His Holy Spirit and the faithful, diligent reading, studying, and memorizing of God's holy, inspired Word. We can do nothing in our own strength. No revival ever came to any person, church, or nation without genuine, fervent prayer and full surrender to God's will.

God's Word encourages us to pray sincerely. "The earnest prayer of a righteous man," James said, "has great power and wonderful results" (James 5:16, TLB). The apostle Paul said, "[God] is a rewarder of those who *diligently* seek Him" (Hebrews 11:6, NKJ). The Lord tells us again in Jeremiah 29:13, "You will seek me and find me when you seek me with *all your heart.*"

I encourage you to dedicate yourself to fasting, prayer, and the Word of God. Pray for yourself, your family, your friends. Ask God to send revival to your church; pray for your pastor and his staff. Pray for other Christian leaders across our land. In all your prayers, be diligent, seeking God with all your heart.

Sixth, *invite God to use you.* Ask Him to show you how to influence your community. Ask Him for a vision for the world. Share your faith in Christ as a way of life to everyone who will listen. Take the initiative to share verbally; the silent witness of a righteous life is not enough. It will not win many, if any, people to Christ. However, a successful verbal witness is always based on a holy life.

Praying for America

Pat Robertson says, "We may be ridiculed by the liberals, but we are the very people who keep judgment from falling on this land." Intercessory prayer for our country is a vital link in this process.

Now that you have humbled yourself and diligently sought the Lord for your own renewal, begin to pray for America. Confess the sins of our nation to God. Intercede for the millions of Americans who are enslaved by sin. In the name of Jesus, rebuke the evil mindset that is gripping the people of America. Pray for our nation's leaders.

Dr. Charles Stanley, pastor of the First Baptist Church of Atlanta, suggests ten ways to pray for the top leaders of America.

- Pray that they will realize their personal sinfulness and their need for cleansing from sin by Jesus Christ.

- Pray that they will recognize their personal inadequacy to fulfill their tasks and that they will depend upon God for knowledge, wisdom, and the courage to do what is right.

- Pray that they will reject all counsel that violates spiritual principles and that they will trust God to prove them right.

- Pray that they will resist those who would pressure them to violate their conscience.

- Pray that they will reverse the trends of socialism and humanism in this nation.

- Pray that they will be willing to sacrifice their own ambitions and political careers for the sake of our nation if necessary.

- Pray that they will rely upon prayer and the Word of God as the source of their daily strength, wisdom, and courage.

- Pray that they will restore dignity, honor, trustworthiness, and righteousness to the office they hold.

- Pray that they will be good examples of conduct to people of our nation.

- Pray that they realize their accountability to Almighty God for the decisions they make.[6]

Unless our nation returns to God—from the top down, where our laws are made—permanent change will be extremely difficult.

However, you can make a big difference. My beloved friend, the late Arthur S. DeMoss, once said: "The transformation of a nation begins on a personal level."[7] Your fasting and praying is the key to the coming revival in America.

A Prayer for Revival

Father God, we come before Your throne to humble ourselves and pray, to seek Your face and turn from our wicked ways.

We have sinned against You, O Lord. We have disobeyed Your clear commands. We have not loved You with all of our heart, soul, mind, and strength. We have not loved our neighbors as we love ourselves.

Forgive us, O God. Heal our land. Send a spirit of repentance. Let it sweep across this nation. Let the purging fire of revival begin in my heart and in Your Church. Let it spread through every community, every town, and every city in America and around the world.

Establish righteousness, we pray. Let the bad roots that produce the bad fruits be burned out of our lives. Father, we ask that godly leaders would be raised up and elected to public office at every level. And that ungodly leaders will be removed. May Satan's hold on government be broken and righteous rule be established. May Your kingdom come and Your will be done on earth as it is in heaven.

This prayer we persistently pray in the name of Jesus and for the glory of God. Amen.

Prayer given by Thomas Trask, general superintendent of the General Council of the Assemblies of God, during a fasting and prayer conference December 5–7, 1994, in Orlando, Florida.

Dynamic Keys to Revival

How to Experience and Maintain Personal Revival

1. Ask the Holy Spirit to reveal any unconfessed sin in your life.

2. Seek forgiveness from all whom you have offended, and forgive all who have hurt you. Make restitution where God leads.

3. Examine your motives in every word and deed. Ask the Lord to search and cleanse your heart daily.

4. Ask the Holy Spirit to guard your walk against complacency and mediocrity.

5. Praise and give thanks to God continually and in all ways on all days, regardless of your circumstances.

6. Refuse to obey your carnal (worldly) nature (Galatians 5:16,17).

7. Surrender your life to Jesus Christ as your Savior and Lord. Develop utter dependence on Him with total submission and humility.

8. Study the attributes of God.

9. Hunger and thirst after righteousness (Matthew 5:6).

10. Love God with all of your heart, soul, and mind (Deuteronomy 6:5).

11. Appropriate the continual fullness and control of the Holy Spirit by faith on the basis of God's *command* (Ephesians 5:18) and *promise* (1 John 5:14,15).

12. Read, study, meditate on, and memorize God's holy, inspired, inerrant Word daily (Colossians 3:16).

13. Pray without ceasing (1 Thessalonians 5:17).

14. Fast and pray one 24-hour period each week. Prayerfully consider becoming one of the two million Christians who will fast for forty days before the end of the year 2000.

15. Seek to share Christ daily as a way of life.

16. Determine to live a holy, godly life of obedience and faith.

17. Start or join a home or church Bible study group that emphasizes revival and a holy life.

How to Experience and Maintain Revival in Your Church

1. Encourage your pastor and church leaders to preach and teach on the attributes of God as a basis for first love, faith, and obedience.

2. Organize a 24-hour prayer chain divided into 96 fifteen-minute periods. Ask participants to fast and pray for revival among church members and for a great spiritual harvest of new believers.

3. Choose seven church members to meet with the pastor early each Sunday morning for prayer and to receive prayer requests for each day of the week.

4. Invite several church members to gather for prayer during each church service, especially while the pastor is preaching or teaching.

5. Encourage all church members to fast and pray on behalf of the pastor and the church one 24-hour period each week.

6. As a pastor or church leader, emphasize biblical truths on repentance, confession of sin, restitution, and reconciliation among church members.

7. Teach members how to be filled and walk in the fullness and power of the Holy Spirit by faith as a way of life.

8. Train members on an ongoing basis to share their faith more effectively in the power of the Holy Spirit.

9. Designate one night each week for positive, aggressive evangelism as a part of church visitation.

10. Challenge members to help fulfill the Great Commission in their neighborhood and have a vision for the world. Since God's great heart is world evangelism, He

will especially bless the church that has a major emphasis on helping to fulfill the Great Commission. Designate a sizeable percentage of the church budget to evangelism outside the United States.

11. Encourage members to honor the Lord through obedient and faithful stewardship. Teach them the joy of giving tithes and offerings. God always blesses a church with a strong missions emphasis. Stress funding for evangelism and discipleship to foreign missions.

12. Teach the history and conditions of revival. Ask members to read biblical and historical accounts of revival.

How to Encourage and Sustain Revival in America

1. Organize prayer groups in homes and churches to fast and pray for revival and to study biblical and historical examples of revival.

2. Encourage publishers, owners, and managers of the Christian print media across America to emphasize fasting and prayer for revival.

3. Encourage all pastors and religious leaders, especially those with access to the electronic and print media, to devote 50 percent of their messages and articles to some facet of revival.

4. Pray specifically for conversion and revival for all who have influence over others in politics, from the precinct to the White House; in education, at all levels of faculty and students; in religion; in all branches of the military; in athletics; in the broadcast and print media; in the entertainment industry—television, film, music, and the arts; in advertising, business, finance, industry, labor, medicine, law, and in other professional areas.

5. Emphasize our biblical, Judeo-Christian roots and American heritage in churches, schools, and civic organizations.

6. Encourage Christian broadcasters to present quality prime-time programs on fasting, prayer, and revival on secular and Christian radio and television stations.

7. Encourage more aggressive efforts to present the "most joyful news" to every nonbeliever in America while at the same time presenting the message of revival to believers.

8. Enlist nationally-known Christian leaders in entertainment, athletics, business, and politics to take leadership in communicating the message of fasting and prayer for revival across America.

How to Lead Your Congregation in a Fast

Dr. Julio C. Ruibal

Most Christians are willing to fast if properly motivated and taught. In this book, Dr. Bright has talked about the spiritual and physical aspects of fasting and prayer. Let me give you some guidelines on how to call your congregation to a corporate time of fasting and prayer.

First, *prepare your congregation for a fast.* Explain the spiritual benefits of fasting and why your church needs to fast as a corporate body. Show from the Scripture how the people of God fasted for direction, protection, deliverance, or spiritual endurance. Inform your congregation of specific needs in your church, city, or the nation for which to fast and pray.

A congregational fasting and prayer gathering should always be initiated and directed by the pastor and leadership of the church. Individuals should not act alone in calling such an event. Not every need or crisis warrants congregational fasting, but certain occasions will arise when a corporate gathering is necessary. The present condition of our nation, for example, is such that we need to call all Christians to fast and pray.

Second, *set a specific time for corporate fasting.* You may wish to set aside one to three days, possibly a week, as the Lord leads. Usually, it is best to start with a shorter period.

I suggest beginning the special convocation on Sunday. Hold meetings each night for intercession, prayer, and supplication.

You may wish to hold early morning prayer gatherings as well. Many working men and women may prefer this time because of other commitments. Mid-morning and early afternoon meetings may provide more suitable opportunity for homemakers with young children. Be sure to provide nursery care for children under school age.

Ask your congregation to choose the times most suited to their schedules. Encourage them to set other activities aside, if possible, to devote themselves to fasting and prayer during this period.

Third, *give your congregation clear instructions*. Provide helpful material on the spiritual and physical aspects of fasting. Be specific about how to begin a fast, what to do during the fast, and how to break it. This information is available in chapters 8 through 10 of this book.

Most people would fast if they understood how natural it is to the body. Often we do not feel like eating. This is common when we suffer from a cold or fever, the flu, or an upset stomach. When extremely tired or experiencing emotional pain, we sometimes go without a meal. But our Western cultures have made us think that abstinence is not good and may even be harmful. Explain to your congregation that no one will die after fasting a day or two. Encourage them to try fasting even if at first it means skipping only a meal or two. Any amount or type of fasting is progress in the right direction. Explain that discomfort is natural and encourage them to persevere.

Describe the different types of fasts mentioned in this book and invite them to choose one or any combination of them.

Fourth, *focus on prayer*. Begin the meeting with a short time of general worship and a brief message of encouragement and instruction. Divide your congregation into small groups, perhaps six to eight at the most, for extended periods of prayer.

You may wish to invite a special speaker to teach on humiliation and brokenness before God or some other aspect of fasting and prayer. But do not lose the dynamic of people sharing and praying in smaller groups. Periodically, invite members of the congregation to share what God is speaking to them. This will encourage others to continue seeking the Lord.

Fifth, *set up a temporary hotline.* Those in your congregation who are fasting may be uncertain how to fast or what they should pray for. Staff the hotline with someone who is experienced in fasting and can encourage fasters and share prayer needs. If a hotline is not possible, appoint someone in your church office to handle the calls.

Sixth, *do not expect everyone to attend every day.* As a rule, you will have a group that will come faithfully each night. Many of your people, however, may not be able to attend every service because of other commitments. Encourage them to fast and pray at home when they cannot come to the church. Be sure to congratulate even the smallest effort made.

Seventh, *teach your people to expect results.* Never have God's people been disappointed when they have fasted and prayed with a pure heart and godly motives. In my church we fast at least once at the beginning of the new year. Often we hold fasting and prayer gatherings on other occasions during the year as well. Always we have witnessed extraordinary results in individual lives, in the ministry, and in our city.

Be prepared to start a revival of major proportion in your church or community. Hundreds, even thousands, may come to the Lord. Your former "dead weight" church members may get on fire for God and start asking you for more opportunities for ministry. Your church's financial situation may improve so much you will have surplus funds to invest in missions. Your staff and lay leaders may ask for more responsibilities and perform their ministries with more zeal and dedication to the Lord. This could well free you to spend more time in prayer and the Word as did the apostles of the Early Church. There is nothing God cannot do through a church that is willing to humble itself before Him.

Our greatest spiritual victories are won on our knees and with empty stomachs. A congregation that can be called to fast and pray is an extraordinary gift to any pastor and to the Church at large.

Additional information on this subject may be obtained from:

> Julio C. Ruibal Foundation
> P.O. Box 1830
> Pinellas Park, FL 34664-1830

Health By Design: Therapeutic Fasting

D. J. Scott, D.M., N.D., D.C.

Therapeutic fasting is the most powerful God-designed tool for the recovery of our health. Its usefulness came built into the very fabric of our life by the wisdom of His design.

I invite you to look with me at a therapy that is applicable in a multitude of diseases. It is just as up-to-date today as it was five thousand years ago and just as consistent with life as breathing, yet it is free of iatrogenic (doctor caused) complications.

Fasting Not New

Fasting dates back to antiquity. Apart from Scripture, the earliest records of therapeutic fasting go back to the ancient civilizations of Greece and the Near East. Plato and Socrates fasted for physical and mental efficiency. The Egyptians resolved syphilis with therapeutic fasting. The renowned Greek physician Hippocrates recognized therapeutic fasting as of primary importance in disease.

In the sixteenth century, a famous Swiss physician Paracelsus said, "Fasting is the greatest remedy." In the seventeenth century, Dr. Hoffman wrote a book, *Description of the Magnificent Results Obtained Through Fasting in All Diseases.* A century later Dr. Von Seeland of Russia wrote that "fasting is a therapeutic of the highest degree possible."

Likewise Dr. Adolph Mayer of Germany wrote, "Fasting is the most efficient means of correcting any disease." Also Dr. Moeller wrote that "fasting is the only natural evolutionary method whereby through a systemic cleansing you can restore yourself by degrees to physiological normality."[1]

Hundreds of brilliant scholars have contributed to modern scientific research into the exact physiological characteristics of fasting. Many hundreds of scientific papers have been published on the subject.

Over the last two centuries, well-known physicians have prescribed therapeutic fasting here in America. One could reasonably estimate that collectively a million or more such fasts have been conducted under supervision. This therapy has been used in almost every disease known.

The Laws of Nature

God built into human flesh physical laws of nature, which if obeyed, will bring into our lives great blessings of health. But if we defy these laws, then we become cursed (diseased) by our own disobedience.

Corrupting our flesh with poisonous products was never intended by the Creator of life as a means of maintaining life. As believers our bodies are not yet spiritual. Dedicated to the spiritual Kingdom of God, our physical bodies are still subject to the physical laws of nature; they can be corrupted or kept healthier by our choices.

Physically, fasting provides one more evidence of God's forgiveness at work as we watch corrupted human flesh transformed back to health through regenerative healing.

No Food in Any Form

Therapeutic fasting does not just mean zero calorie intake; it means no food at all—in any form. Only pure water intake is permitted. Christians today mistakenly believe that Christ and the prophets of old possessed supernatural powers to go forty days without food. Not so. In my practice, I see Christians and non-Christians alike do this routinely.

Nutrition is fundamentally necessary; nothing living can be sustained without it. Food, however, is not nutrition; it is the raw material of nutrition. Food must be digested, absorbed, transported, modified, and utilized to be nutrition. (This requires a multitude of precisely integrated physiological processes. One human cell—and there are trillions in each of us—is more complex than the universe in which we live. Only God could design such a magnificent mechanism wherein every single cell is consistently working toward harmonious health.)

Fasting is never starvation. Starvation is rapidly fatal because nutrients are not available. Never for one moment in the fast is the organism deprived of essential nutrients. These are quickly remobilized from internal resources.

The Advantage of Fasting

Fasting promotes nutritional reorganization. Livers repair, stomachs heal, intestines gain tone. Hardly a tissue goes without benefit from nutritional regeneration during the fast.

Regeneration is the term we use to describe healing and repair. This quality is so tremendously enhanced in a fast that many diseases which never subside while one is eating quickly heal during the fast.

Fasting can help one regain his youthfulness. At the University of Chicago, Carlson and Kunde placed a forty-year-old male on a two-week fast and discovered that his cellular physiology was that of a seventeen-year-old. These benefits are acquired by ridding the cells of toxic metabolic accumulants.

Another amazing characteristic of fasting is autolysis—the ability of the organism to self-digest and remove unwanted material and accumulations from the body without touching vital structures. Autolysis is a normal quality of physiology, but in fasting it becomes greatly enhanced so that many tumors, cysts, abscesses, abnormal accumulations, and fatty deposits are completely or largely absorbed.

Food is one of our biggest workloads on all systems, but especially on the heart and circulation. Stopping all food not only puts the entire intestinal track at rest, but the heart and most other organs as well. Add physical rest to this life support system and we see most serious conditions regenerate to improved health in extended fasts.

Uncomfortable symptoms that may develop during the fast are evidence of increased elimination of toxic metabolic waste. Very bad breath, terrible tastes in the mouth, body odors, foul discharges, eruptions on the skin, diarrhea, and vomiting frequently become indicators. These increased eliminations subside as the body removes the offending toxins and diseases.

Hormone imbalances are often corrected in the fast. This is more obvious in the young female who may be infertile or suffering from amenorrhea. Commonly we see menstrual cycles restored after only two to three weeks of fasting. A number of sterile couples have been able to conceive following a fast. Impotent males are not an uncommon occurrence in our society. These folks are most grateful when they can recover normal marital relationships.

Therapeutic fasting also benefits the mind. The brain is the organ of the mind just as surely as the heart is the central organ of circulation. Brain chemistry affects the mind. If your mind is upset, first look at how you are poisoning your brain. People consume food additives, drugs, and substances to which they are sensitive or allergic. These may cause brain chemistry alterations with seriously disturbing mental consequences. These substances must be totally removed from our internal environment if our brain chemistry is to return to normal. This is why we see uncontrollable moods, intolerable feelings, abysmal depression, and mental confusions return to normal even while fasting. The vast majority of mental aberrations, I believe, are physiological rather than psychological in nature.

Avoid Drugs

During a fast, avoid all drugs, homeopathic remedies, and even natural herbal drugs. The body best does its own work of defense and repair unhampered by the suppression of its repair activities. Drugs, along with various toxic remedies, are generally dangerous during a fast. With few exceptions, their dosage could be very fragile.

The insulin-dependent diabetic may have to be under the care of a diabetologist. Here again, the dosage would have to be adjusted very carefully. While the ocular pressure in glaucoma drops during a fast, to remove medication prematurely and without monitoring could result in blindness. Some drugs such as steroids have to be withdrawn gradually. Asthmatics, even the worst lifetime cases, can be drug free usually in a few days to a week or so. As a chiropractic physician, I insist that medication must first be withdrawn by the medical physician in charge or with his or her supervision during the fast.

Fasting Is Safe

The physician periodically doing blood profiles during the fast attempts to clearly track quantitatively and therefore physiologically almost every organ, system, and disease process while one is recovering.

The great advantage of this evaluation is that it clearly defines safety during the fast.

Therapeutic fasting should be done under professional supervision only. The quality of experienced, well-trained professional supervision is vitally important. The physician must qualify first by total dedication to the inherent wisdom of God's design. He must shun all forms of toxic assault that are intended only to relieve unpleasant symptoms. Many symptomatic remedies are toxic agents and should only be resorted to where the doctor believes there is a life-threatening emergency.

Change in Lifestyle

I never supervise anyone on a fast who is not totally committed to a lifestyle of normal living thereafter. If you intend to go back to conventional eating—high-fat, high-protein foods (meat, cheese, butter, milk, eggs, ice cream); seasonings, tea, coffee; refined, processed, or denatured foods along with those many foods that contain an abundance of female hormones and carcinogenic agents—then most certainly your diseases will all return. Like the New Testament character who swept his house clean, the demons all left, but when they returned they brought their many friends to occupy a cleaned up dwelling. That man's last state was worse than his first.

Why indulge in the "demons" (foodstuffs) of death that God never designed to arrive on our tables in the way they have been commercially altered today?

These simple truths are available to those who have been allowed to learn through physical suffering. I believe He has enabled me to learn these truths because I value His wisdom above the wisdom of men. I have yet to find in the field of verifiable science where this confidence has been betrayed. Of course, I do consult with other physicians and refer to other specialists when a problem is outside my appropriate care. Gratefully the vast majority of human health problems can be greatly improved by simple lifestyle changes. Sometimes this includes fasting.

Condensed from Dr. Scott's original article on this subject. His unabridged version can by requested by writing to Dr. D. J. Scott, 17023 Lorain Ave., Cleveland, OH 44111. Dr. Scott is an internationally-recognized and respected expert on supervised fasting and an avid proponent of natural hygiene. He is the founding president of the International Association of Professional Natural Hygienists and director of Scott's Natural Health Institute in Strongsville, Ohio, which he founded in 1957.

Releasing God's Supernatural Power

Discover the Secret of Successful Prayer

The story is told of a man who traveled to a certain city one cold morning. As he arrived at his hotel, he noticed that the clerks, the guests—everyone—was barefooted. In the coffee shop, he noticed an attractive fellow at a nearby table and asked, "Why aren't you wearing shoes? Don't you know about shoes?"

"Of course I know about shoes," the patron replied.

"Then why don't you wear them?" the visitor asked.

"Ah, that is the question," the patron returned. "Why don't I wear shoes?"

After breakfast, the visitor walked out of the hotel and into the snow. Again, every person he saw was barefooted. Curious, he asked a passerby, "Why doesn't anyone here wear shoes? Don't you know that they protect the feet from the cold?"

The passerby said, "We know about shoes. See that building? It's a shoe factory. We are so proud of the plant that we gather there every week to hear the man in charge tell us how wonderful shoes are."

"Then why don't you wear shoes?" the visitor persisted.

"Ah, that is the question," the passerby replied. "Why don't we wear shoes?"

When it comes to prayer, many Christians are like the people in that city. They know about prayer, they believe in its power, they frequently hear sermons on the subject, but it is not a vital part of their lives.

In my study of God's Word and in my travels throughout the world, I have become absolutely convinced that wherever people really pray according to biblical principles, God works in their lives and through them in the lives of others in a special way. Show me a church or a Christian organization that emphasizes prayer, and I'll show you a ministry where people are excited about Jesus Christ and are witnessing for Him. On the other hand, show me a church or Christian cause where there is little emphasis on prayer, and I will show you worldly Christians who have little interest in the souls of men and women. Their lives can best be described by the experience of the Church of Ephesus (Revelation 2) and the Church of Laodicea (Revelation 3).

As we consider the secret of successful prayer, let me answer six vital questions.

What Is Prayer?

Simply put, prayer is communicating with God. As a child of God you are invited to come boldly before His throne. "Since we have a great high priest who has gone through the heavens, Jesus the Son of God," the apostle Paul writes, "...let us then approach the throne of grace with confidence, so that we may receive mercy and find grace to help us in our time of need" (Hebrews 4:14–16).

Because of who God is—the King of kings and the Lord of lords, the Creator of heaven and earth—we must come into His presence with reverence. But He is also our loving heavenly Father who cares for us and delights in having fellowship with us. Therefore, we can come to Him with a reverent, joyful heart, knowing that He loves us more than anyone else has ever loved us or will ever love us.

Someone has said, "Prayer is the creator as well as the channel of devotion. The spirit of devotion is the spirit of prayer. Prayer and devotion are united as soul and body are united, as life and heart are united. There is no real prayer without devotion, no devotion without prayer." Real prayer is expressing our devotion to our heavenly Father, inviting Him to talk to us as we talk to Him.

Who Can Pray?

Anyone can pray, but only those who walk in faith and obedience to Christ can expect to receive answers to their prayers. Jesus says, "I am the way and the truth and the life. No one comes to the Father except through me" (John 14:6). Contact with God begins when we receive Jesus into our lives as Savior and Lord.

Praying with a clean heart is also vital to successful prayer. The psalmist says, "If I had cherished sin in my heart, the Lord would not have listened" (Psalm 66:18). We cannot expect God to answer our prayers if there is any unconfessed sin in our life.

One of the most frequent hindrances to prayer is an unforgiving spirit. Jesus says, "When you stand praying, if you hold anything against anyone, forgive him, so that your Father in heaven may forgive you your sins" (Mark 11:25). No prayer except the prayer of confession can be answered by God unless it comes from a heart that is free of unforgiveness and bitterness. You and I must come to God with a forgiving heart if we are to receive the Christian's legacy of power in prayer.

In addition, we must have a believing heart if we expect God to answer our prayers. Jesus says, "If you believe, you will receive whatever you ask for in prayer" (Matthew 21:22), and "According to your faith will it be done to you" (Matthew 9:29). Yet few of us take these words seriously, and few dare to claim what God has so generously promised us.

Why Are We to Pray?

God commands us to pray. The New Testament commands to pray are many. Here are a few: Watch and pray (Luke 21:36; Mark 14:38). Pray with thanksgiving (Philippians 4:6; Colossians 4:2). Pray in the Spirit (1 Corinthians 14:15). Always pray and not give up (Luke 18:1).

We also pray to have fellowship with God. Prayer is not just an "escape hatch" for us to get out of trouble, please ourselves, or gain our selfish ends. It is our "hotline" of communication and fellowship with God. In the process, we receive spiritual nurture and strength to live a victorious life, and we maintain the boldness necessary for a vital witness for Christ.

Genuine, biblically-based prayer does change things. It so transforms those who pray that God is free to reveal His will to them. Prayer also releases God's great power to change the course of nature, people, and nations. The faithful prayers of Spirit-filled believers have proven this throughout the Bible and history.

To Whom Do We Pray?

We pray to the Father in the name of the Lord Jesus Christ through the ministry of the Holy Spirit. When we pray to the Father, our prayers are accepted by Jesus Christ and interpreted to God the Father by the Holy Spirit.

But because God is one God, manifested in three persons, and since there is no jealously between the three persons of the Trinity, it is perfectly acceptable to pray to Jesus or to the Holy Spirit.

As we pray, both Jesus and the Holy Spirit are interceding on our behalf. Paul records in Romans 8:34, "Christ Jesus, who died—more than that, who was raised to life—is at the right hand of God and is also interceding for us." Earlier in that chapter, Paul wrote, "The Spirit helps us in our weakness...And he who searches our hearts knows the mind of the Spirit, because the Spirit intercedes for the saints in accordance with God's will" (verses 26,27).

When Should We Pray?

God's Word commands us to "Pray continually" (1 Thessalonians 5:17).

Charles Spurgeon said, "Prayer pulls the rope down below, and the great bell rings above in the ears of God. Some scarcely stir the bell, for they pray so languidly; others give only an occasional jerk at the rope. But he who communicates with heaven is the man who grasps the rope boldly and pulls continuously with all his might."

We can be in prayer frequently throughout the day, demonstrating our devotion to God as we go about our daily tasks.

I have found it meaningful to begin every morning in prayer. As I get out of bed, I fall on my knees to worship Him as a way of saying, "Lord, I bow before You and acknowledge You as my Master."

Throughout the day, I focus my thoughts on the Lord, often talking to Him, praising Him, and thanking Him for His goodness, love, and grace in my behalf. I pray for wisdom about the numerous decisions I must make each day. I pray for the salvation of friends and strangers, the healing of the sick, and the spiritual and material needs of Campus Crusade for Christ and other ministries. I even pray that the way I dress, as well as my words and actions, will bring glory to God. I ask Him to think with my mind, to love with my heart, and to speak with my lips. Since He came to seek and to save the lost, I ask Him to seek and to save the lost through me.

In the evening I ask, "Lord, is there anything in me that is displeasing to You, anything I need to confess?" If the Holy Spirit reveals any sins or weaknesses, I confess them and claim by faith God's victory for my life. I then like to spend time reading and meditating on God's Word so that my subconscious thoughts are on the Lord Jesus all during the night.

It is not always necessary to be on our knees, or even in a quiet room to pray. God wants us to be in touch with Him constantly wherever we are. We can pray in the car, while washing the dishes, or while walking down the street. The more frequently we share our thoughts and desires with our Lord, the more meaningful our fellowship and the closer we come to Him.

What Should We Include in Our Prayers?

Although prayer cannot be reduced to a formula, certain basic elements should be included in our communication with God—*Adoration, Confession, Thanksgiving, Supplication* (ACTS).

A—Adoration

To adore God is to worship and praise Him, to honor and exalt Him in our heart and mind and with our lips. The Word of God teaches that our Father desires the fellowship of His children, of which adoration is a vital part (John 4:23,24; Hebrews 12:28). Adoration expresses our complete trust in Him and reflects our confidence that He hears us. Adoration demonstrates our reverence, awe, love, and gratitude.

C—Confession

When our discipline of prayer begins with adoration, the Holy Spirit has opportunity to reveal any sin in our life that needs to be confessed. By seeing God in His purity, His holiness, and His love, we become aware of our sinfulness and unworthiness. Confessing our sin and receiving His forgiveness restores us to fellowship with Him and clears the channel for God to hear and answer our prayers (1 John 1:7–9).

T—Thanksgiving

Nothing pleases God more than our consistent expression of faith. What better way to do this than to tell Him, "Thank You"? God's Word commands, "Give thanks in all circumstances, for this is God's will for you in Christ Jesus" (1 Thessalonians 5:18). An attitude of thanksgiving enables us to recognize that God controls all things—not just the blessings, but the problems and adversities as well. As we approach God with a thankful heart, He becomes strong on our behalf; conversely, a critical, unbelieving spirit displeases God and hinders His efforts to bless and enrich us and to use us for His glory.

S—Supplication

Supplication includes petition for our own needs and intercession for others. We are to pray for everything and in specific terms.

As you talk to God, for example, pray that your inner person may be renewed, always sensitive to and empowered by the Holy Spirit. Pray about your problems, pray for wisdom and guidance, pray for strength to resist temptation, pray for comfort in time of sorrow—pray for everything (Philippians 4:6).

Then pray for others—your spouse, your children, your parents, neighbors, and friends. Pray for your pastor and missionaries, and for various other Christians to whom God has given special responsibility. Pray for those in authority over you (1 Timothy 2:1,2).

Pray especially for the salvation of souls, for a daily opportunity to introduce others to Christ and to the ministry of the Holy Spirit, and for the fulfillment of the Great Commission (1 Timothy 2:3,4). Begin with your campus or your community. Pray for and seek to find one or more Christian friends with whom you can establish prayer partnerships (Matthew 18:19).

These elements—adoration, confession, thanksgiving, and supplication—have helped many Christians to develop a more well-rounded prayer life.

Experience the Power of the Holy Spirit

A dear friend, Dee Jepsen, wife of former U.S. Senator Roger Jepsen, attended a luncheon in the Senate Caucus Room on Capitol Hill in Washington, D.C.

Congressmen, Cabinet members, top leaders in government, and many other respected guests were seated in the impressive room with its ornate pillars, high ceilings, and huge chandeliers. The room seemed to swell with influential people who had gathered to honor a humble servant of God.

Then Mother Teresa entered the room.

Mrs. Jepsen said, "She looked so tiny and out-of-place in her blue-and-white habit, old gray sweater, and sandals that had obviously carried her many miles. The room and prestigious guests seemed to dwarf her."

Immediately the top leaders of the most powerful country in the world along with the other esteemed guests rose to their feet and applauded. Many had tears in their eyes.

"I was struck with the contrast," Mrs. Jepsen said. "I thought, *Lord, this frail woman has more power than I see in the Halls of Congress. She reflects Jesus everywhere she goes, and everyone is strangely moved.*"

Mother Teresa doesn't own anything; she has never asked for material possessions nor held up her fist to demand rights for herself. Yet she has been raised to a pinnacle of recognition for her work with the destitute and dying in Calcutta, India. She has reached down into the gutter and loved those whom the world has called unlovable. A shining example of selflessness, she proves the power of God's love to transform people and touch a starved world.

This is real power and, unlike that of the world, it confounds the wise and humbles the mighty. It is the power of God working through ordinary men and women for His glory.

Perhaps you are wondering, *Why isn't my Christian life more exciting and fulfilling? How can I receive power to live victoriously and be a fruitful witness for the Lord Jesus?*

Jesus promised, "I have come that they [you and I and all Christians] may have life, and that they may have it more abundantly" (John 10:10, NKJ). Yet, if you are an average professing Christian, you are undoubtedly thinking, *There is certainly nothing abundant about my life. I try to witness, but no one is interested in what I have to say. I experience nothing but doubts, fears, frustrations, and defeat. Surely there must be something more to this Christian life, but I have never found it.*

There was a time in my own Christian ministry when I challenged Christians to witness and live holy lives for Christ, but the results were so discouraging that I began to devote most of my time and energies to evangelism, where God blessed with much more apparent results. However, as the years have passed, the Holy Spirit has helped me to see the great potential power in lukewarm Christians, if only they are awakened and harnessed for Christ.

I am now convinced that lukewarm, worldly Christians can be changed into vital, dynamic, witnesses if they will surrender their wills to Christ, be filled with the Holy Spirit, and receive training in evangelism and discipleship.

The Difference
Again and again I am reminded of the great contrast between the Church of Jesus Christ today and His Church of the first century.

Some theologians would say that it is the degree of commitment. But many people all over the world are crying out to God, dedicating their lives to Christ day after day, yet they continue to live spiritually impotent and defeated lives.

Why? Are we not told in Matthew 5:6, "Blessed are those who hunger and thirst for righteousness, for they will be filled"?

Did not John, the beloved disciple, quote Jesus (1 John 1:5–7) as saying that God is light, and in Him is no darkness at all, and that if we walk in the "light" we have fellowship with the Father and the Son?

We need not live in spiritual poverty. The many thousands of promises recorded in the Word of God apply to every Christian. These promises include: assurance of God's love (John 3:16); eternal life (Romans 6:23); forgiveness of sin (1 John 1:9); provision of material needs (Philippians 4:19); the ordering of one's steps (Psalms 37:23); the secret of successful prayer (John 15:7); promise of an abundant life (John 10:10); God's promise to honor a holy life (2 Chronicles 16:9); assurance that everything that happens is for our own good (Romans 8:28); deliverance from temptation (1 Corinthians 10:13); victory over fear (1 John 4:18); and thousands of others.

The Bible promises that every Christian can possess love, joy, peace, faith, and many other beneficial qualities. What is wrong? Why is the average Christian not experiencing this quality of life?

Dr. Billy Graham has said that, according to his research, at least 90 percent of all Christians in America are living defeated lives. Others who are in a position to know the spiritual pulse of America have made similar statements.

It is quite likely that, according to the law of averages, you are among that 90 percent. You may have a heart for God. You read your Bible faithfully, you pray, you witness, you are active in your church; yet year after year you continue to fight a losing battle. Temptations come. Half-heartedly you resist, then yield, surrendering until you are finally defeated. For months you journey in the slough of despondency like Mr. Christian in John Bunyan's *Pilgrim's Progress*. Then you attend a spiritual retreat and you are back on the

Alpine heights for a brief time. Up, down, victories, defeats! Soon you cry out with Paul in Romans 7:24, "What a wretched man I am! Who will rescue me from this body of death?"

As president of Campus Crusade for Christ, it has been my privilege to speak to many thousands of students each year since 1951. At the conclusion of a message that I gave at Princeton University, a devout young man approached me to express his great concern over his lack of "fruit" in witnessing. "I read my Bible for an hour. I pray for an hour, and I witness for an hour each day," he said. "I attend every Christian meeting on campus. Yet, I have never been able to introduce another to Christ. What's wrong with me?" In counseling with him, I gently probed for the answer to his problem. I knew that he meant business. He wanted to please God. He sincerely wanted his friends to know his wonderful Savior, and, according to his conduct and Christian activities, he was a model Christian.

Jesus promises in John 14:26 and 16:13 that the Holy Spirit will teach us all things and will guide us into all truth. As I counseled with this young man, we were directed to several very important passages of Scripture that explain the person and ministry of the Holy Spirit. I shared how he could be filled with the Holy Spirit by faith based on God's *command* to be filled (Ephesians 5:18) and God's *promise* that if we ask for anything according to His will, He would hear and answer (1 John 5:14,15). When he claimed the fullness of the Holy Spirit by faith, God unlocked the door to victory and to unspeakable joy.

The young man left the counseling room rejoicing and with an expectant heart. At that point, he began to experience a fruitful life in Christ such as he had never before known. He knew that something had happened in his life. He was a new man—no longer afraid, spiritually impotent, and defeated. Now he was bold and had power and faith to believe God. He could hardly wait to see what God was going to do through him.

"Lord," he prayed, "who will be the first You will lead me to today?"

In the course of the day, the Holy Spirit led this young Christian to a fellow student to whom he had previously witnessed without apparent success. But today was different. God had prepared the heart of the other student, and soon these two were bowed in prayer as the student friend received Christ. The next day this marvelous experience was repeated with another student responding as if drawn by an invisible hand.

This is not strange, for the Word of God tells us, "No one can come to me unless the Father who sent me draws him" (John 6:44). Through the power of the Holy Spirit, this Princeton student continued to lead fellow students to Christ day after day. His own life was so wonderfully changed and empowered, so used of God, that he eventually became a minister.

Each of us must be filled with the Holy Spirit to be an effective witness for Christ:

> You will receive power when the Holy Spirit comes on you; and you will be my witnesses in Jerusalem, and in all Judea and Samaria, and to the ends of the earth (Acts 1:8).

Every biblical reference to the filling of the Holy Spirit, in both the Old Testament and the New Testament, relates to power for service and witness.

Beginning with the day of Pentecost and continuing through the centuries, the work of God has always been accomplished through men and women who were filled with the Holy Spirit—men such as Peter, Paul, and all the disciples.

In more recent times, men like John Wesley, Jonathan Edwards, Charles Finney, Dwight L. Moody, Charles Spurgeon, G. Campbell Morgan, R. A. Torrey, Billy Graham, and scores of other Christian leaders who have been filled with the Holy Spirit have been greatly used to further the cause of Christ and His kingdom. However, the filling of the Holy Spirit is not limited to Christian leaders, but is available to each of us who meets God's terms.

Hear what some of these men and women of God say about the importance of every Christian being filled with the Holy Spirit:

> Men ought to seek with their whole hearts to be filled with the Spirit of God. Without being filled with the Spirit, it is utterly impossible that an individual Christian or a church can ever live or work as God desires. — *Andrew Murray*

> Christians are as guilty for not being filled with the Holy Spirit as sinners are for not repenting. They are even more so, for as they have more light, they are so much the more guilty. — *Charles G. Finney*

> The Spirit-filled life, that life that permits His fullness in a sustained overflow, is the only life that can please God. — *Norman B. Harrison*

> The great purpose in the filling of the Holy Spirit is power for service. The best and most-used Christians known to me have been men who have testified to a deeper experience of the filling of the Holy Spirit.
> — *J. Edwin Orr*

> I believe that it is impossible for any Christian to be effective either in his life or in his service unless he is filled with the Holy Spirit who is God's only provision of power. —*Henrietta C. Mears*

> Read the biographies of God's men and you will discover that each one sought and obtained the endowment of power from on high. One sermon preached in the anointing is worth a thousand in the energy of the flesh. —*Dr. Oswald J. Smith*

I wish to make it especially clear that the Holy Spirit already dwells within every believer and the special power that attends the filling of the Holy Spirit is not reserved for Christian leaders alone. Every Christian not only has the prerogative of being filled with the Holy Spirit, but is also admonished to be filled with the Spirit (Ephesians 5:18). Therefore, if a Christian is not filled, he is disobedient to the command of God and is sinning against Him. Further, since God commands us in His Word to be filled with the Spirit, we may be certain that He has the power to fill us the very moment we invite Him to do so.

What Is the Spirit-Filled Life?

The Spirit-filled life is the Christ-filled life. The Spirit-filled Christian is one who, according to Romans 6:11, considers himself dead to sin, but alive to God in Christ Jesus. The One who has been given "all authority in heaven and on earth" (Matthew 28:18) and in whom "all the fullness of the Deity lives in bodily form" (Colossians 2:9) can now express that power through the Spirit-filled believer. The One who came to seek and to save the lost now begins to seek the lost through the Christian. He directs the Christian's steps to those who are lost and to those who are in need. He begins to use the Christian's lips to tell of His love. His great heart of compassion becomes evident in the life of the Spirit-filled Christian.

In a very real sense, the Christian gives up his life, his spiritual impotence, defeat, and fruitlessness for the power and victory of Jesus Christ. This is what the great missionary statesman Hudson Taylor referred to as the "exchanged life."

When we are filled with the Holy Spirit, we are filled with Jesus Christ. We no longer think of Christ as One who helps us do some kind of Christian task but, rather, Jesus Christ does the work through us. Christ does not want us to work for Him. He wants us to let Him do His work in and through us. This is the glorious experience that the apostle Paul knew when he said in Galatians 2:20, "I have been crucified with Christ and I no longer live, but Christ lives in me." Our body now becomes Christ's body to use as He wills; our mind becomes His mind to think His thoughts; our will is now controlled by His will; our total personality, time, and talents are now completely His.

Paul goes on to say, "The life I live in the body, I live by faith in the Son of God, who loved me and gave himself for me." Faith in whom? Faith in the Son of God, the One who loved us and gave Himself for us, the One who has been given "all authority in heaven and on earth."

Think of it! Can you grasp what this means?

If you yield your will to God the Holy Spirit and acknowledge that Jesus Christ is in fact in your life moment by moment, you are in for a great adventure. The Lord Jesus Christ will begin to draw scores of lost men and women to Himself through your yielded, Spirit-filled life.

What Results Can You Expect From Being Filled With the Holy Spirit?

Now comes the real test that will determine if you are truly filled with the Holy Spirit. Do you find that you have a greater love for Christ? Are you more concerned for those who do not know His love and forgiveness? Are you experiencing a greater faith, boldness, liberty, and power in witnessing? If so, you are filled with the Spirit. Jesus Christ is beginning to express His life and love through and in you.

Remember, Jesus promised that we would receive power after the Holy Spirit has come upon us. After receiving power we will naturally want to be His witnesses wherever we are (Acts 1:8).

It is definitely true that you will have a greater love for Christ, for your fellow man, and for the Word of God when you are filled with the Holy Spirit. As Paul said in Romans 5:5, "God has poured out his love into our hearts by the

Holy Spirit, whom he has given us." Also, the fruit of the Spirit—love, joy, peace, patience, kindness, goodness, faithfulness, gentleness, and self-control (Galatians 5:22,23)—will become more evident in your life.

However, there is a difference between the fruit of the Spirit and the gifts of the Spirit.

The filling of the Holy Spirit is given for power and boldness in witnessing for Christ. Most Christian leaders agree with Dr. R. A. Torrey who said:

> I have gone through my Bible time and time again checking this subject and I make this statement without the slightest fear of successful contradiction that there is not one single passage in the Old Testament or the New Testament where the filling with the Holy Spirit is spoken of, where it is not connected with testimony for service.

As a Christian abides in Christ, living in the fullness of the Spirit, the fruit of the Spirit is developed and the Christian becomes more mature spiritually.

The maturing of the fruit of the Spirit is a lifetime process that goes on continually as Christ-like characteristics are being formed in the life of the Christian. Some Christians give greater evidence of the fruit of the Spirit than do others because of a greater degree of yieldedness to His working.

The more we acknowledge ourselves to be dead to sin and give allegiance to the Lord Jesus Christ and His life within us, and the more we allow Him through the power of the Holy Spirit to live out His life through us, the more evident will be the fruit of the Spirit.

Although the development and maturing of the fruit of the Spirit is a long process, the gifts of the Holy Spirit are given at the time a person becomes a Christian. Though every believer who is filled with the Spirit receives power for witnessing, not every Christian receives the same gift, according to 1 Corinthians 12. Some are called to be apostles, some prophets, others evangelists, pastors, and teachers

(Ephesians 4:11). Therefore, we must let the Lord direct us into the place of service He has for us.

Do not imitate the ministry of someone else. Be patient. Do not decide what you should do with your life or where you should serve Christ. He will express His life in and through you as you continue to study His Word and remain obedient and sensitive to the leading of the Holy Spirit. Through God's Word, the direction of the Holy Spirit, and the wise counsel of mature Christians, you will discover what God's will is for you.

As you ask God to fill you with the Holy Spirit by faith, you are about to begin the greatest adventure of your life. Remember that you are asking to be filled with the Holy Spirit rather than with self. As He takes control of your life, you will become more like Christ. The Holy Spirit is not the author of confusion and emotional extremes. He has come to exalt and glorify Jesus; therefore, when you are filled with the Holy Spirit, it will be your constant desire to do the will of God and that which will please and honor Jesus Christ.

Why did Jesus come into this world? "To seek and to save what was lost" (Luke 19:10).

What will please Him most? We please Him most as we help fulfill His Great Commission by going into all the world and preaching the gospel to every creature by inviting Him to live His life through us, beginning in our "Jerusalem."

How is this to be accomplished? Through the power of the Holy Spirit.

Think of it—you and I are privileged to be used by our risen, indwelling Savior to help reach a lost world with the glorious Good News!

Have You Made the Wonderful Discovery of the Spirit-Filled Life?

Every day can be an exciting adventure for the Christian who knows the reality of being filled with the Holy Spirit and who lives constantly, moment by moment, under His gracious direction.

The Bible tells us that there are three kinds of people:

1. Natural Man: One who has not received Christ.

"A natural man does not accept the things of the Spirit of God; for they are foolishness to him, and he cannot understand them, because they are spiritually appraised" (1 Corinthians 2:14, NASB).

Self-Directed Life
S – Self is on the throne
† – Christ is outside the life
● – Interests are directed by self, often resulting in discord and frustration

2. Spiritual Man: One who is directed and empowered by the Holy Spirit.

"He who is spiritual appraises all things" (1 Corinthians 2:15, NASB).

Christ-Directed Life
S – Christ is in the life and on the throne
† – Self is yielding to Christ
● – Interests are directed by Christ, resulting in harmony with God's plan

3. Carnal Man: One who has received Christ, but who lives in defeat because he trusts in his own efforts to live the Christian life.

"I, brethren, could not speak to you as to spiritual people but as to carnal, as to babes in Christ. I fed you with milk and not with solid

Self-Directed Life

S – Self is on the throne

† – Christ dethroned and not allowed to direct the life

● – Interests are directed by self, often resulting in discord and frustration

food; for until now you were not able to receive it, and even now you are still not able; for you are still carnal. For when there are envy, strife, and divisions among you, are you not carnal and behaving like mere men?" (1 Corinthians 3:1–3).

The following are four principles for living the Spirit-filled life:

 God has provided for us an abundant and fruitful Christian life.

"Jesus said, 'I have come that they may have life, and that they may have it more abundantly' " (John 10:10, NKJ).

"I am the vine, you are the branches. He who abides in Me, and I in him, bears much fruit; for without Me you can do nothing" (John 15:5, NKJ).

"The fruit of the Spirit is love, joy, peace, patience, kindness, goodness, faithfulness, gentleness, self-control; against such things there is no law" (Galatians 5:22,23).

"You shall receive power when the Holy Spirit has come upon you; and you shall be My witnesses both in Jerusalem, and in all Judea and Samaria, and even to the remotest part of the earth" (Acts 1:8).

The following are some personal traits of the spiritual man that result from trusting God:

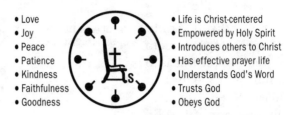

- Love
- Joy
- Peace
- Patience
- Kindness
- Faithfulness
- Goodness

- Life is Christ-centered
- Empowered by Holy Spirit
- Introduces others to Christ
- Has effective prayer life
- Understands God's Word
- Trusts God
- Obeys God

The degree to which these traits are manifested in the life depends on the extent to which the Christian trusts the Lord with every detail of his life, and on his maturity in Christ. One who is only beginning to understand the ministry of the Holy Spirit should not be discouraged if he is not as fruitful as more mature Christians who have known and experienced this truth for a longer period.

Why is it that most Christians are not experiencing the abundant life?

2 Carnal Christians cannot experience the abundant and fruitful Christian life.

The carnal man trusts in his own efforts to live the Christian life:

- He is either uninformed about, or has forgotten, God's love, forgiveness, and power (Romans 5:8–10; Hebrews 10:1–25; 1 John 1; 2:1–3; 2 Peter 1:9; Acts 1:8).

- He has an up-and-down spiritual experience.

- He cannot understand himself—he wants to do what is right, but cannot.

- He fails to draw on the power of the Holy Spirit to live the Christian life (1 Corinthians 3:1–3; Romans 7:15–24; 8:7; Galatians 5:16–18).

Some or all of the following traits may characterize the carnal man—the Christian who does not fully trust God:

- Legalistic attitude
- Impure thoughts
- Jealousy
- Guilt
- Worry
- Discouragement
- Critical spirit
- Frustration

- Aimlessness
- Fear
- Ignorance of his spiritual heritage
- Unbelief
- Disobedience
- Loss of love for God and for others
- Poor prayer life
- No desire for Bible study

(The individual who professes to be a Christian but who continues to practice sin should realize that he may not be a Christian at all, according to 1 John 2:3; 3:6–9; Ephesians 5:5.)

The third truth gives us the only solution to this problem...

3 Jesus promised the abundant and fruitful life as the result of being filled (directed and empowered) by the Holy Spirit.

The Spirit-filled life is the Christ-directed life by which Christ lives His life in and through us in the power of the Holy Spirit (John 15).

■ One becomes a Christian through the ministry of the Holy Spirit, according to John 3:1–8. From the moment of spiritual birth, the Christian is indwelt by the Holy Spirit at all times (John 1:12; Colossians 2:9,10; John 14:16,17).

Though all Christians are indwelt by the Holy Spirit, not all Christians are filled (directed and empowered) by the Holy Spirit on an ongoing basis.

■ The Holy Spirit is the source of the overflowing life (John 7:37–39).

■ The Holy Spirit came to glorify Christ (John 16:1–15). When one is filled with the Holy Spirit, he is a true disciple of Christ.

- In His last command before His ascension, Christ promised the power of the Holy Spirit to enable us to be witnesses for Him (Acts 1:1–9).

How, then, can one be filled with the Holy Spirit?

4 We are filled (directed and empowered) by the Holy Spirit by faith; then we can experience the abundant and fruitful life that Christ promised to each Christian.

You can appropriate the filling of the Holy Spirit right now if you:

- Sincerely desire to be directed and empowered by the Holy Spirit (Matthew 5:6; John 7:37–39).

- Confess your sins. By faith, thank God that He has forgiven all of your sins—past, present, and future—because Christ died for you (Colossians 2:13–15; 1 John 1; 2:1–3; Hebrews 10:1–17).

- Present every area of your life to God (Romans 12:1,2).

- By faith claim the fullness of the Holy Spirit, according to:

  His command: Be filled with the Spirit. "Do not get drunk on wine, which leads to debauchery. Instead, be filled with the Spirit" (Ephesians 5:18).

  His promise: He will always answer when we pray according to His will. "This is the confidence we have in approaching God: that if we ask anything according to his will, he hears us. And if we know that He hears us—whatever we ask—we know that we have what we asked of Him" (1 John 5:14,15).

Faith can be expressed through prayer...

How to Pray in Faith to be Filled With the Holy Spirit

We are filled with the Holy Spirit by faith alone. However, true prayer is one way of expressing your faith. The following is a suggested prayer:

> Dear Father, I need You. I acknowledge that I have been directing my own life and that, as a result, I have sinned against You. I thank You that You have forgiven my sins through Christ's death on the cross for me. I now invite Christ to again take His place on the throne of my life. Fill me with the Holy Spirit as You commanded me to be filled, and as You promised in Your Word that You would do if I asked in faith. I pray this in the name of Jesus. As an expression of my faith, I now thank You for directing my life and for filling me with the Holy Spirit.

Does this prayer express the desire of your heart? If so, bow in prayer and trust God to fill you with the Holy Spirit right now.

How to Know That You Are Filled (Directed and Empowered) By the Holy Spirit

Did you ask God to fill you with the Holy Spirit? Do you know that you are now filled with the Holy Spirit? On what authority? (On the trustworthiness of God Himself and His Word: Hebrews 11:6; Romans 14:22,23.)

Do not depend on feelings. The promise of God's Word, not our feelings, is our authority. The Christian lives by faith (trust) in the trustworthiness of God Himself and His Word.

This train diagram illustrates the relationship among *fact* (God and His Word), *faith* (our trust in God and His Word), and *feeling* (the result of our faith and obedience) (John 14:21).

The train will run with or without the caboose. However, it would be futile to attempt to pull the train by the caboose. In the same way, we as Christians do not depend on feelings or emotions, but we place our faith (trust) in the trustworthiness of God and the promises of His Word.

How to Walk in the Spirit

Faith (trust in God and His promises) is the only means by which a Christian can live the Spirit-directed life.

If you become aware of an area of your life (an attitude or an action) that is displeasing to the Lord, even though you are walking with Him and sincerely desiring to serve Him, simply thank God that He has forgiven your sins—past, present, and future—on the basis of Christ's death on the cross. Claim His love and forgiveness by faith and continue to have fellowship with Him.

If you retake the throne of your life through sin—a definite act of disobedience—breathe spiritually.

Spiritual breathing (exhaling the impure and inhaling the pure) is an exercise in faith and enables you to experience God's love and forgiveness.

1. *Exhale*—confess your sin—agree with God concerning your sin and thank Him for His forgiveness of it, according to 1 John 1:9 and Hebrews 10:1–25. Confession involves repentance—a change in attitude and action.

2. *Inhale*—surrender the control of your life to Christ, and appropriate (receive) the fullness of the Holy Spirit by faith. Trust that He now directs and empowers you, according to the *command* of Ephesians 5:18 and the *promise* of 1 John 5:14,15.

This is an adaptation of the popular Campus Crusade for Christ booklet designed to help Christians share with other believers the joy of Spirit-controlled living. You may obtain copies of this booklet at Christian bookstores, through your mail-order catalog distributor, or from NewLife Publications.

Would You Like to Know God Personally?

If you have never placed your faith in the God of our Founding Fathers, the God who has revealed Himself in the Holy Scriptures, I encourage you to do so now.

You can know God personally, as presumptuous as that may sound. God is so eager to establish a personal, loving relationship with you that He has already made all the arrangements. He is patiently and lovingly waiting for you to respond to His invitation. You can receive forgiveness of your sin and assurance of eternal life through faith in His only Son, the Lord Jesus Christ.

The major barrier that prevents us from knowing God personally is ignorance of who God is and what He has done for us. The following four principles will help you discover how to know God personally and experience the abundant life He promised.

 God **loves** you and created you to know Him personally.

(References should be read in context from the Bible wherever possible.)

God's Love

"God so loved the world that he gave his one and only Son, that whoever believes in Him shall not perish, but have eternal life" (John 3:16).

God's Plan

"This is eternal life: that they may know you, the only true God, and Jesus Christ, whom you have sent" (John 17:3).

What prevents us from knowing God personally?

2 Man is **sinful** and **separated** from God, so we cannot know Him personally or experience His love.

Man Is Sinful

"All have sinned and fall short of the glory of God" (Romans 3:23).

Man was created to have fellowship with God; but, because of his own stubborn self-will, he chose to go his own independent way and fellowship with God was broken. This self-will, characterized by an attitude of active rebellion or passive indifference, is an evidence of what the Bible calls sin.

Man Is Separated

"The wages of sin is death" [spiritual separation from God] (Romans 6:23).

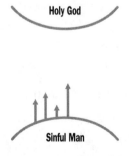

This diagram illustrates that God is holy and man is sinful. A great gulf separates the two. The arrows illustrate that man is continually trying to reach God and establish a personal relationship with Him through his own efforts, such as a good life, philosophy, or religion—but he inevitably fails.

The third principle explains the only way to bridge this gulf...

3 Jesus Christ is God's **only** provision for man's sin. Through Him alone we can know God personally and experience God's love.

He Died In Our Place

"God demonstrates his own love for us in this: While we were still sinners, Christ died for us" (Romans 5:8).

He Rose From the Dead

"Christ died for our sins... he was buried... he was raised on the third day according to the Scriptures... he appeared to Peter, and then to the Twelve. After that, he appeared to more than five hundred..." (1 Corinthians 15:3–6).

He Is the Only Way to God

"Jesus answered, 'I am the way and the truth and the life. No one comes to the Father except through me'" (John 14:6).

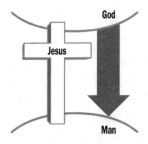

This diagram illustrates that God has bridged the gulf that separates us from Him by sending His Son, Jesus Christ, to die on the cross in our place to pay the penalty for our sins.

It is not enough just to know these truths...

We must individually **receive** Jesus Christ as Savior and Lord; then we can know God personally and experience His love.

We Must Receive Christ

"To all who receive him, to those who believed in his name, he gave the right to become children of God" (John 1:12).

We Receive Christ Through Faith

"By grace you have been saved, through faith—and this not from yourselves, it is the gift of God—not by works, so that no one can boast" (Ephesians 2:8,9).

When We Receive Christ, We Experience a New Birth

(Read John 3:1–8.)

We Receive Christ By Personal Invitation

[Christ speaking] "Behold, I stand at the door and knock; if anyone hears My voice and opens the door, I will come in to him" (Revelation 3:20, NASB).

Receiving Christ involves turning to God from self (repentance) and trusting Christ to come into our lives to forgive us of our sins and to make us what He wants us to be. Just to agree intellectually that Jesus Christ is the Son of God and that He died on the cross for our sins is not enough. Nor is it enough to have an emotional experience. We receive Jesus Christ by faith, as an act of our will.

These two circles represent two kinds of lives:

Self-Directed Life
S – Self is on the throne
† – Christ is outside the life
● – Interests are directed by self, often resulting in discord and frustration

Christ-Directed Life
† – Christ is in the life and on the throne
S – Self is yielding to Christ
● – Interests are directed by Christ, resulting in harmony with God's plan

Which circle best represents your life?

Which circle would you like to have represent your life?

The following explains how you can receive Christ:

You Can Receive Christ Right Now By Faith Through Prayer
(Prayer is talking with God)

God knows your heart and is not so concerned with your words as He is with the attitude of your heart. The following is a suggested prayer:

> Lord Jesus, I want to know You personally. Thank You for dying on the cross for my sins. I open the door of my life and receive You as my Savior and Lord. Thank You for forgiving me of my sins and giving me eternal life. Take control of the throne of my life. Make me the kind of person You want me to be.

Does this prayer express the desire of your heart?

If it does, pray this prayer right now, and Christ will come into your life, as He promised.

How to Know That Christ Is in Your Life

Did you receive Christ into your life? According to His promise in Revelation 3:20, where is Christ right now in relation to you? Christ said that He would come into your life and be your friend so you can know Him personally. Would He mislead you? On what authority do you know that God has answered your prayer? (The trustworthiness of God Himself and His Word.)

The Bible Promises Eternal Life to All Who Receive Christ

> "This is the testimony: God has given us eternal life, and this life is in his Son. He who has the Son has life; he who does not have the Son of God does not have life. I write these things to you who believe in the name of the Son of God so that you may know that you have eternal life" (1 John 5:11–13).

Thank God often that Christ is in your life and that He will never leave you (Hebrews 13:5). You can know on the basis of His promise that Christ lives in you and that you have eternal life from the very moment you invite Him in. He will not deceive you.

An important reminder...

Do Not Depend on Feelings

The promise of God's Word, the Bible—not our feelings—is our authority. The Christian lives by faith (trust) in the trustworthiness of God Himself and His Word. This train diagram illustrates the relationship among *fact* (God and His Word), *faith* (our trust in God and His Word), and *feeling* (the result of our faith and obedience) (John 14:21).

The train will run with or without the caboose. However, it would be useless to attempt to pull the train by the caboose. In the same way, we as Christians do not depend on feelings or emotions, but we place our faith (trust) in the trustworthiness of God and the promises of His Word.

Now That You Have Entered Into a Personal Relationship With Christ

The moment you received Christ by faith, as an act of your will, many things happened, including the following:

1. Christ came into your life (Revelation 3:20 and Colossians 1:27).

2. Your sins were forgiven (Colossians 1:14).

3. You became a child of God (John 1:12).

4. You received eternal life (John 5:24).

5. You began the great adventure for which God created you (John 10:10; 2 Corinthians 5:17; and 1 Thessalonians 5:18).

Can you think of anything more wonderful that could happen to you than entering into a personal relationship with Jesus Christ? Would you like to thank God in prayer right now for what He has done for you? By thanking God, you demonstrate your faith.

To enjoy your new relationship with God...

Suggestions for Christian Growth

Spiritual growth results from trusting Jesus Christ. "The righteous man shall live by faith" (Galatians 3:11). A life of faith will enable you to trust God increasingly with every detail of your life, and to practice the following:

G *Go* to God in prayer daily (John 15:7).

R *Read* God's Word daily (Acts 17:11)—begin with the Gospel of John.

O *Obey* God moment by moment (John 14:21).

W *Witness* for Christ by your life and words (Matthew 4:19; John 15:8).

T *Trust* God for every detail of your life (1 Peter 5:7).

H *Holy Spirit*—Allow Him to control and empower your daily life and witness (Galatians 5:16,17; Acts 1:8).

Fellowship in a Good Church

God's Word admonishes us not to forsake "the assembling of ourselves together" (Hebrews 10:25). Several logs burn brightly together, but put one aside on the cold hearth and the fire goes out. So it is with your relationship with other Christians. If you do not belong to a church, do not wait to be invited. Take the initiative; call the pastor of a nearby church where Christ is honored and His Word is preached. Start this week, and make plans to attend regularly.

This is a version of the popular *Four Spiritual Laws* and was designed to help Christians share their faith in Jesus Christ as a way of life. You may obtain copies of this booklet at Christian bookstores, through your mail-order catalog distributor, or from NewLife Publications.

Source Notes

Preface

1. E. E. Shelhamer, *How to Experience Revival* (Springdale, PA: Whitaker House, 1984), p.7.

Chapter 1

1. "America in a Bad Mood, Poll Shows," Associated Press, *Orlando Sentinel*, September 21, 1994.

Chapter 2

1. Henry T. Blackaby and Claude V. King, *Experiencing God* (Nashville: Broadman & Holman Publishers, 1994), p.31.

2. The invitation committee included: Joe Aldrich, Neil Anderson, Kay Arthur, George Barna, Henry Blackaby, Richard Bott, Bill and Vonette Bright, David Bryant, Larry Burkett, Luis Bush, Paul Cedar, Charles Colson, Paul Crouch, Evelyn Christenson, W. A. Criswell, Roger Cross, Loren Cunningham, James and Shirley Dobson, Steve Douglass, Dick Eastman, Howard Edington, Ted Engstrom, Paul Eshleman, Tony Evans, Bill Gothard, Brandt Gustavson, Richard Halverson, David Hannah, Jack Hayford, Stephen Hayner, Howard Hendricks, Jim Henry, E. V. Hill, John Holland, John Howe, Marvin Kehler, D. James Kennedy, Jerry Kirk, Tim and Beverly LaHaye, Greg Laurie, Max Lucado, James MacKnight, E. Bailey Marks, Peter Marshall, Bill McCartney, Tom Moffit Jr., Alberto Mottesi, Richard Mouw, Lloyd Ogilvie, Luis Palau, Bill Pickett, Pat Robertson, Adrian Rogers, Mark Rutland, Denny Rydberg, Al Sanders, Robert Schuller, Robert Seiple, Dal Shealy, Charles Smith, Neil Snyder, Charles Stanley, Vinson Synan, Thomas Trask, C. Peter Wagner, Thomas Wang, Jerry White, Luder Whitlock, Ralph Winter, and Ed Young.

Chapter 3

1. "Robinson Angered, His Speech With Religious References Canceled By Sarasota Schools," *Jet*, June 20, 1994, p.23.

2. William J. Bennett, *The Devaluing of America, the Fight for Our Culture and Our Children* (New York: Summit Books, 1992), pp.204,205.

3. Bennett, p.211.

4. Cal Thomas, "Rediscovering Right, Wrong—We've Got to Restore Standards," *Los Angeles Times Syndicate*, published in *The Orlando Sentinel*, November 2, 1994, p.A19.

5. Kathryn Stechert Black, "Reading, Writing and Weapons," *Woman's Day*, Vol. 1, Issue 14, Section 1, 1993, p.75.

6. Bridget Murray, "Human Nature, Attitudes and Age," *Psychology Today*, April/May 1993, p.96.

7. "Human Nature, Attitudes and Age," *Psychology Today*, p.96.

8. "Reading, Writing and Weapons," *Woman's Day*, p.76.

9. "Human Nature, Attitudes and Age," *Psychology Today*, p.96.

10. "Reading, Writing and Weapons," *Woman's Day*, p.78.

11. Celia W. Dugger, "Youthful, Impressionable and Accused of Murder," *The New York Times*, May 17, 1994, p.A1, final edition.

12. Statement made during a fasting and prayer gathering December 5–7, 1994, in Orlando, Florida.

13. Susan Chira, "Study Confirms Some Fears on U.S. Children," *The New York Times*, April 12, 1994, p.A1.

14. Nancy R. Gibbs, "Bringing Up Father," *Time*, June 28, 1993, p.53.

15. Armand Nicholi Jr., contributor to *Family Building* by George Rekers (Ventura, CA: Gospel Light Publications, 1985), cited in "The Fractured Family," *The Rebirth of America*, published by the Arthur S. DeMoss Foundation, 1986, p.93.

16. "The Fractured Family," *The Rebirth of America*, p.95.

17. "Bringing Up Father," *Time*, p.55.

18. Allan Bloom, *The Closing of the American Mind* (New York: Simon and Schuster, 1987), pp.82,83.

19. Bloom, p.117.

20. Bloom, p.118.

21. Bloom, p.118.

22. David Larsen, "The Christian's Resources in the Local Church," in John Woodbridge (ed.), *Renewing Your Mind in a Secular World* (Chicago: Moody Press, 1985), pp.73,74.

23. Mark A. Noll, *A History of Christianity in the United States and Canada* (Grand Rapids: Wm. B. Eerdmans, 1992), pp.452,453.

24. "More Than 4,000 Rally in Support of Fired Principal Who Let Students Pray," *Jet*, December 20, 1993, pp.6–10.

25. "More Than 4,000 Rally in Support of Fired Principal…" *Jet*, pp.4–10.

26. *Stone v. Graham*, 449 U.S. 39 (1980).

27. "Man Sues to Ban the Ten Commandments," *Charlotte Observer*, cited in *The Orlando Sentinel*, November 19, 1994, p.A-14.

28. George Barna, *The Future of the American Family* (Chicago: Moody Press, 1993), p.153.

Chapter 4

1. George Barna, *The Frog in the Kettle* (Ventura, CA: Regal Books, 1990), pp.22,23.

2. **Fellowship in a Good Church**
   God's Word admonishes us not to forsake "the assembling of ourselves together" (Hebrews 10:25). Several logs burn brightly together, but put one aside on the cold hearth and the fire goes out. So it is with your relationship to other Christians. If you do not belong to a church, do not wait to be invited. Take the initiative; call the pastor of a nearby church where Christ is honored and His Word is preached. Start this week, and make plans to attend regularly.

   (Taken from page 15 of the *Four Spiritual Laws.*)

3. George Barna, *The Future of the American Family* (Chicago: Moody Press, 1993), pp.67,68.

4. Barna, *The Frog in the Kettle*, p.65.

5. Barna, *The Future of the American Family*, p.71.

6. Billy Graham, *Storm Warning* (Dallas: Word Publishing, 1992), p.28.

7. Graham, p.28.

8. Graham, p.29.

9. Graham, p.30.

10. Barna, *The Frog in the Kettle*, p.23.

Chapter 5

1. Winkie Pratney, *Revival* (Springdale, PA: Whitaker House, 1984), p.189.

2. Pratney, p.190.

3. Pratney, p.188.

4. Winkie Pratney, *Revival: Its Principles & Personalities* (LaFayette, LA: Huntington House, 1994), p.17.

5. David L. McKenna, *The Coming Great Awakening* (Downers Grove, IL: InterVarsity Press, 1990), p.30.

6. Pratney, *Revival: Its Principles & Personalities*, p.31.

7. Pratney, p.29.

8. Pratney, p.26

9. Pratney, p.26.

10. George Wallis, *In the Day of Thy Power* (Fort Washington, PA: Christian Literature Crusade, 1956), p.84.

11. J. Edwin Orr, *The Event of the Century* (Wheaton: International Awakening Press, 1989), p.275.

12. Orr, pp.274–76.

13. Pratney, *Revival: Its Principles & Personalities*, p.17.

14. J. Edwin Orr, excerpted from *The Role of Prayer in Spiritual Awakening,* a video produced by Campus Crusade for Christ.

15. McKenna, *The Coming Great Awakening*, p.31.

16. Pratney, *Revival: Its Principles & Personalities*, p.32.

17. Orr, *The Role of Prayer in Spiritual Awakening* video.

Chapter 6

1. Arthur Wallis, *God's Chosen Fast* (Fort Washington, PA: Christian Literature Crusade, 1993), p.50.
2. Wallis, p.47.
3. Lee Bueno, *Fast Your Way to Health: A Guide to Physical Healing and Spiritual Enrichment* (Springdale, PA: Whitaker House, 1991), p.201.
4. Comment made during a fasting and prayer conference December 5–7, 1994, in Orlando, Florida.
5. Andrew Murray, cited by Arthur Wallis, *God's Chosen Fast*, p.50.
6. Bueno, p.201.
7. Bueno, p.199.
8. Adam Clarke, *Clarke's Commentary* (Nashville: Abingdon, n.d.), p.411.
9. Norman Grubb, *Rees Howells: Intercessor* (Fort Washington, PA: Christian Literature Crusade), p.55.
10. Wallis, *God's Chosen Fast*, p.82.
11. Wallis, p.82.
12. Wallis, pp.51,52.
13. Wallis, p.13.
14. Derek Prince, *Fasting* (Springdale, PA: Whitaker House, 1986), p.35.

Chapter 7

1. Richard J. Foster, *Celebration of Discipline* (San Francisco: HarperSanFrancisco, 1988), p.50.
2. Derek Prince, *Fasting* (Springdale, PA: Whitaker House, 1986), pp.44,45.
3. Foster, p.50.
4. Adapted from Bob Rodgers, *101 Reasons to Fast*, (Louisville, KY: Evangel Christian Life Center, 1994), p.7.
5. Foster, p.50.
6. Prince, p.43.
7. Arthur Wallis, *God's Chosen Fast* (Fort Washington, PA: Christian Literature Crusade, 1993), p.56.
8. Wallis, p.58.

Chapter 8

1. David R. Smith, *Fasting: A Neglected Discipline* (Fort Washington, PA: Christian Literature Crusade, 1969), p.6.
2. Derek Prince, *Fasting* (Springdale, PA: Whitaker House, 1986), p.15.
3. Richard J. Foster, *Celebration of Discipline* (San Francisco: HarperSanFrancisco, 1988), p.47.
4. 1 Kings 21:9; Nehemiah 9:1; Esther 4:3; 9:31; Psalm 35:13; 109:24; Isaiah 58:3,4,6; Jeremiah 36:6,9; Daniel 9:3; Joel 2:12; Matthew 4:2; 6:16,18; Mark 2:18; Luke 2:37; Acts 13:2; 14:23.

5. Prince, pp.11–13.

6. Edith Schaeffer, *The Life of Prayer* (Wheaton: Crossway Books, 1992), p.75.

7. Smith, p.6.

8. Smith, p.21.

9. Smith, p.23.

10. Smith, p.24.

11. Foster, p.55.

12. Schaeffer, pp.75,76.

13. Wesley L. Duewel, *Touch the World Through Prayer* (Grand Rapids: Francis Asbury Press, 1986), p.97.

14. Foster, p.55.

15. Foster, p.54.

16. Foster, p.55.

17. R. D. Chatham, *Fasting: A Biblical-Historical Study* (South Plainfield, NJ: Bridge Publishing, 1987), pp.152,153.

18. Chatham, p.149.

19. Smith, p.73.

20. Foster, p.51.

21. Lee Bueno, *Fast Your Way to Health* (Springdale, PA: Whitaker House, 1991), p.77.

22. See Bueno, *Fast Your Way to Health* and Paul C. Bragg, *The Miracle of Fasting* (Santa Barbara, CA: Health Science, n.d.).

23. Allan Cott, M.D., *Fasting: The Ultimate Diet* (New York: Bantam Books Inc., 1975), p.63. See also Bueno, pp.257,258.

24. Bueno, p.250.

25. Foster, p.49.

26. Bueno, p.61.

27. According to Dr. Julio Ruibal of the Julio Ruibal Foundation, Pinellas Park, Florida.

28. Foster, p.57.

29. Foster, p.49.

30. Foster, p.50.

31. Arthur Wallis, *God's Chosen Fast* (Fort Washington, PA: Christian Literature Crusade, 1993), p.142.

32. Bueno, p.150.

33. Bragg, p.80; Bueno, pp.85–96.

34. From comments on fasting provided after a conference on prayer and fasting December 5–7, 1994, in Orlando, Florida.

Chapter 9

1. Unpublished manuscript. Copyright Evelyn Christensen Ministries. Used by permission.

2. Lee Bueno, *Fast Your Way to Health* (Springdale, PA: Whitaker House, 1991), p.207.

3. James F. Balch, M.D., and Phyllis A. Balch, C.N.C., *Prescription for Nutritional Healing* (Garden City Park, NY: Avery Publishing Group Inc., 1990), p.325.

4. Balch, p.325.

5. Pamela Smith, *Charisma* magazine, May 1992, p.100.

6. Balch, p.328.

7. Bueno, pp.85–93.

8. Balch, p.325.

9. Balch, p.325.

10. Dr. Julio Ruibal's suggestions are only brief and general guidelines for fasting. For more information on fasting by Dr. Ruibal, write the Julio C. Ruibal Foundation, P.O. Box 1830, Pinellas Park, FL 34664-1830 or call (813) 524-8386.

Chapter 10

1. Dr. Julio Ruibal.

2. See Paul C. Bragg, *The Miracle of Fasting* (Santa Barbara, CA: Health Science, n.d.), p.82; and Arthur Wallis, *God's Chosen Fast* (Fort Washington, PA: Christian Literature Crusade, 1993), p.143.

3. Lee Bueno, *Fast Your Way to Health* (Springdale, PA: Whitaker House, 1991), pp.74,75.

4. Bueno, pp.74–76,101.

5. Ruibal.

6. Pamela Smith, *Charisma* magazine, May 1992, p.100.

7. Richard Foster, *Celebration of Discipline* (San Francisco: HarperSanFrancisco, 1988) pp.57,58.

8. Bueno, p.70.

9. Bragg, p.75.

10. Smith, p.100.

11. Dr. Julio Ruibal's comments were presented during a fasting and prayer gathering December 5–7, 1994, in Orlando, Florida.

12. Ruibal.

Chapter 11

1. John Price, "May God Heal Our Land," from *America at the Crossroads* (Wheaton: Tyndale House, 1979), cited in *The Rebirth of America*, published by the Arthur S. DeMoss Foundation, 1986, p.155.

2. Pat Robertson, *The Turning Tide* (Dallas: Word Publishing, 1993), p.7.

3. David L. McKenna, *The Coming Great Awakening* (Downers Grove, IL: InterVarsity Press, 1990), pp.17,18.

4. George Barna, *The Frog in the Kettle* (Ventura, CA: Regal Books, 1990), p.22.

5. Pat Robertson, president of CBN, made this statement during a fasting and prayer conference December 5–7, 1994, in Orlando, Florida.

6. Adapted from "How to Intercede for Influential Men," *The Rebirth of America*, p.193.

7. Arthur S. DeMoss, "How to Be Sure," cited in *The Rebirth of America*, p.175.

Appendix C

1. A. De Vries, *Therapeutic Fasting* (Los Angeles: Chandler Book Co., 1963), p.6.

Resources for Further Reading

Andrews, J. R. *George Whitefield* (Ehricksville, OH: Barbour and Company Inc., 1990).

Barna, George. *Absolute Confusion: The Barna Report* (Ventura, CA: Regal Books, 1994).

Barna, George. *The Frog in the Kettle* (Ventura, CA: Regal Books, 1990).

Barna, George. *Virtual America: The Barna Report* (Ventura, CA: Regal Books, 1994).

Bragg, Paul C. and Patricia. *The Miracle of Fasting* (Santa Barbara, CA: Health Science, n.d.).

Bueno, Lee. *Fast Your Way to Health* (Springdale, PA: Whitaker House, 1991).

Chatham, R. D. *Fasting: A Biblical-Historical Study* (South Plainfield, NJ: Bridge Publishing, 1987).

Duewel, Wesley L. *Touch the World Through Prayer* (Grand Rapids: Francis Asbury Press, 1986).

Foster, Richard J. *Celebration of Discipline* (San Francisco: HarperSanFrancisco, 1988).

Graham, Billy. *Storm Warning* (Dallas: Word Publishing, 1992).

Grubb, Norman. *Rees Howells Intercessor* (Fort Washington, PA: Christian Literature Crusade, 1993).

Lloyd-Jones, Martyn. *Revival* (Wheaton: Crossway Books, 1987).

McKenna, David L. *The Coming Great Awakening* (Downers Grove, IL: InterVarsity Press, 1990).

Pratney, Winkie. *Revival* (Springdale, PA: Whitaker House, 1984).

Pratney, Winkie. *Revival: Its Principles & Personalities* (La-Fayette, LA: Huntington House Publishers, 1986).

Prince, Derek. *Fasting* (Springdale, PA: Whitaker House, 1986).

Ravenhill, Leonard. *Revival God's Way* (Minneapolis: Bethany House Publishers, 1986).

Robertson, Pat. *The Turning Tide* (Dallas: Word Publishing, 1993).

Schaeffer, Edith. *The Life of Prayer* (Wheaton: Crossway Books, 1992).

Smith, David R. *Fasting: A Neglected Discipline* (Fort Washington, PA: Christian Literature Crusade, 1969).

Wallis, Arthur. *God's Chosen Fast* (Fort Washington, PA: Christian Literature Crusade, 1993).

Wesley, John. *The Nature of Holiness*, compiled by Clare George Weakley Jr. (Minneapolis: Bethany House Publishers, 1988).

Wesley, John. *The Nature of Revival*, compiled by Clare George Weakley Jr. (Minneapolis: Bethany House Publishers, 1987).

Response Form

☐ Please send me more information on how to become a Christian.

☐ I have just received Jesus Christ as my Savior and Lord and would appreciate more information on how to experience the abundant Christian life.

☐ Please inform me of other materials on how I can be filled with the Holy Spirit and be more effective in my prayer.

☐ Please send me information on quantity discounts for additional copies of *The Coming Revival* to give to my pastor, church, loved ones, and friends.

Name_____

Address_____

City_____

State_____ Zip_____

Phone (   )_____

Please check the appropriate box(es) and mail this form in an envelope to:

Bill Bright
Campus Crusade for Christ
P.O. Box 593684
Orlando, FL 32859